MY LIFE:
FROM BRIGAND TO KING

MY LIFE:
FROM BRIGAND TO KING

AUTOBIOGRAPHY
OF
AMIR HABIBULLAH

THE OCTAGON PRESS
LONDON

Copyright © 1990 The Octagon Press

ISBN 0 863040 47 0

Published in this edition in 1990

Printed and bound in Great Britain by
The Camelot Press Ltd, Southampton.

A NOTE

THIS remarkable narrative is from the original Persian of Jamal—the brigand and scribe—and was dictated by Bacha Saquo the water-carrier's son himself; who rising from the life of heinous crime, and shaking with his tread at least one part of the East, waded through blood to the proud throne of Afghanistan, till the selfless services of Nadir Shah and his brothers rescued the country from revolution.

Jamal grew up with the Bacha, as a brigand. Following his master's fortune, he was a constant companion of Bacha during the Reign of Terror, as the Afghans call the period before the coming of Nadir Shah. Although Jamal was known by various names, he was nevertheless, not styled by any particular official designation as such, for during the bandit's regime, even highly placed officials changed places almost hourly.

Like so many companions of the Bacha, he too, evaded capture on the fall of the brigand; and escaping decapitation as a traitor, made his way out of the country to ply a humble trade between Europe and the Middle East.

For a time he placed his narrative at the disposal of a Persian-knowing scholar, when Jamal was roaming about in Europe as a Man of no Country. The latter rendered, a somewhat rough and ready original into the English language, without disturbing the essentials. Although it is arguable, whether a brigand, however uncouth, is incapable of using psychological terms, the introduction of some Latin phrases here and there, is excusable for the accommodation of difficult Oriental expressions into more familiar European terminology.

Not only because the translator's name may uselessly intrude and confuse the essential story by dragging in immaterial characters; but also because, being already satisfied with his integrity, we have undertaken to suppress his name due to the nature of his occupation, and to avoid any unnecessary political controversy that it may give rise to.

It is, however, only too natural that some may regard the brigand's narrative as incredible; the reason being that even in the turbulent story of Afghanistan, the Reign of Terror was of such unprecedented horror and abnormality that usual standards cannot be applied to it. For the rest, it can be said that whereas, the work is not an historical encyclopædia, yet dates and facts mentioned in it tally with authoritative data.

FOREWORD BY JAMAL GUL

THE Man Who Would Be King gazed sullenly
into the entrails of a defunct jazail. They lay
around his feet—the long, soft-iron barrel wrenched
from the decorative yet primitive stock, and the
flintlock and other mechanism twisted into unwork-
able distortion. What had been the life and pride
of the water-carrier's son—the structure upon which
his youthful martial ardour was pyramided—had
finished its useful span in inglorious anti-climax.

Disdaining the blood which streamed down his
badly-lacerated face, he who would and was to be
King, allowed his angry gaze to travel over the
sun-scorched boulders to the gory, inanimate mess,
thirty feet away. It was the remains of a mountain
sheep—mainly head and intestines.

The man who was destined to rule Afghanistan
for nine tempestuous months, turned suddenly on
his heel, and addressed me.

"Jamal," he said, "would'st remove that carcase?
. . . The expression is obscene. . . . It reminds me
of thy cousin, Fazal!"

Bacha Saquo was then ten years of age, and we
were scholars in the same village school.

The worthy Mullah, whose unthankful task it
was to impart the rudiments of his culture to the
unruly progeny of our Kohistan highlanders, had
long washed his holy hands of Bacha. I, however,

was in a different category. I was his favourite
pupil in that I proved dexterous with the reed pen
and ox-gall, which served for writing material,
and my memory was such that I could recite long
passages from the Holy Kuran.

Even before this day, marked as it was by the
mutilation of an innocuous and innocent sheep, I
had come under the dominance of Bacha in many a
youthful escapade.

When he addressed me so familiarly, and so
confidently, I forgot that he was merely the son
of the village *saga* (water-carrier), and I saw only
his supreme arrogance.

Then and there I made a resolve. I would hitch
my wagon to this extraordinary person's star. From
thereon, I commenced to write. I became this
King-to-be's shadow.

Little I knew then, as I gazed upon him, open-
mouthed, that he was to drag me through years of
amazing adventure, through periods of hunger and
want, and others of wasteful plenty and licentious-
ness. Little I hazarded then of blood baths, and
debauchery; of swift passes across the hills, and
slashing, murderous attacks upon merchants'
caravans.

It never entered my youthful head that one day
we should be laying siege to the Capital of the
God-gifted Kingdom of Afghanistan, and we should
see those who gainsaid our merest whim disintegrated
before the mouths of cannon.

Not for a fleeting instant did I foresee the time
when we should hold court in the famous Irag
Palace, while the relatives of the ruling House lay

herded like goats in the darkest recesses of Kabul's citadel; and certainly—or perhaps I would have hesitated—did I fail to see that one day I would be an outcast from my native land with a price upon my head.

All I saw then was a precocious boy of ten with a mouth whose thin lips were pressed together in a tight line. That mouth was not made to smile. It was hard and cruel, yet undoubtedly betokening a strong physique and resolute mentality.

The figure, too, was sturdy, with promise of a fine chest, abundant muscle and virile manhood. The hands were strong and supple, and the legs, encased in tattered pyjamas, could grip and stay on anything on four legs. Even then had I seen Bacha astride a maddened buffalo, and I had observed him from the hillside when he had tamed and broken in a young and spirited Yarkandi stallion.

Bacha became my guiding star for good or evil, and I, never entirely divorced from my love of writing, became his scribe.

As Bacha spoke and dictated to me, hiding behind mountain crags, leading his men over the pass, in the thick of battle, in the Irag Palace at Kabul, or in the confines of the condemned cell, so I wrote.

My notes were rough, and were frequently written upon anything that came to hand.

Bearing this in mind, perhaps you will do me the honour to read?

CONTENTS

MY LIFE:

FROM BRIGAND TO KING

CHAPTER I

A VILLAGE IN KOHISTAN

THE hot, pitiless sun beat down on the brown, stony confines of my village in Kohistan. It was a miserable village, and I, Bacha Saquo, had conceived a deep hatred of its poverty-stricken exterior and the self-sufficiency permeated by the Elders who ruled its puny and insignificant destinies.

Twenty-three juvenile heads, within the welcome shade of the mud-walled hovel which was our school, rocked back and forth in lazy, listless unison to the behests of the bearded Mullah, our teacher.

I, Bacha, must intone with the rest, for the watchful eye of my enemy but seldom strayed from my direction. What matter that I knew not what I said? Perforce, I must conform to discipline.

"O, jabee jab . . . O, mamde jab . . . O, yaked jab," we gabbled, some of us who knew not the words merely making discordant sounds to fit the occasion.

Noise—volume—rhythm—was all our mentor demanded, so that the Elders, passing in the village street, could hear the nonsensical chorus, and shake their heads wisely.

I

"The worthy Mullah," they would remark with unction, "is passing on to our sons his manifold gifts."

Noise I was prepared to donate, for more I could not. The ways of the pen and the *kitab* ever remained mysteries to me, perhaps because my thoughts were never within the four walls of that drab, grim school.

More, of course, this Holy man had endeavoured to obtain. He had complained, despairingly, to my father, the water-carrier, and—he had struck me—yes, across the head with his open palm, and across my back with his switch. And—this man was my enemy.

As I sat there, cross-legged, upon the smooth, mud-dung floor, mumming my puny pretence at obedience, my eyes would seek this man's beard. They would peer further, beneath those straggling, hennaed hairs, to the scraggy muscles of that scrawny throat, and my eyes, underneath their film of complacent acquiescence to the dictate of authority, would gleam and smoulder as I imagined my hands at their work, tearing at the windpipe, and playing expertly with the jugular. Yes—I knew the technique. I had not roved the hills for nothing. I had already seen a man die, but that knowledge I kept to myself.

Gazing surreptitiously through the slits in the mud walls which let in both light and air, my thoughts would wander to the mountains and beyond, and I dreamed of what would happen when I came to man's estate.

I, Bacha Saquo, might be the village water-carrier's son, but not for me the *mussack*, and the labour of carrying slopping hides from the well.

In my mind's eye, as I crouched there, intoning, I could discern horsemen upon those shrubless, treeless hills, and the horsemen led pack mules, and heavily laden camels. In the rear, and in the place of honour between the village and a vigilant enemy, would be Bacha, returning victoriously from a descent upon the caravan routes.

Actually, in the haze upon the hilltops, through a slit to the right of the Mullah's head, there was a horseman. My sharp eyes had ferreted him out, though he still sought the cover of the boulders. Soon, he was joined by another, and yet another. Then, camels came into sight, and more horsemen. The man in the van I recognised. I knew the action of his mount, and the poise of its head. The man was a neighbour, who had denied the village his society for the past five days. Undoubtedly, he had done more than repair to the hills to round up the cattle which had strayed—or had they strayed? That, at least, was the story we scholars were told.

"O, yakedyab . . . O, yabeedejab . . . O, jaber-dejab," continued the class, but I forgot to intone.

A slight movement to the left of that intriguing slit arrested and held my attention. The beard—it had ceased its upward and downward motion—an action which always reminded me of the tuft upon a billy-goat's chin moving in synchronism to the animal's munching—and its absurd and irritating longitudinal uprisings and aggravating downcomings had given place to a forward aggressiveness. Slowly, this feeble and unlovely appendage was thrust forward into intolerable belligerency, and my eye travelled upward, past quivering nostrils attached to a beaked, aquiline nose to eyes, rheumy yet wrathful. I started to my feet, giving a little cry, but I was too late. The aged one was upon me, beating with his switch upon the skin which showed all too plentifully through the rents in my much-patched shirt.

My enemy was at work, and I fled incontinently, the shrill raucous cries of my schoolmates following me as I sought the sanctuary of the outer sunshine.

My enemy . . . I, Bacha, had been struck . . . I was but fourteen, but already I did a man's work in the fields and with the herds. . . . And—I had been beaten!

Worse, for the aged one could not hurt, there had been the derisive cries of my schoolfellows. . . .

I, Bacha, would be avenged.

.   .   .   .   .

It was Friday, the day of Prayer and of meditation, and the Mullah must needs be at the mosque. Consequently, there was no school.

I, Bacha, had the boys before me—Emir Din, the son of the chandler, Fazl Haq, the son of the carrier, Jamal Gul, the light of the Mullah's eyes, and a score of others.

Answering the thrice-given cry of the jackal—for such was my private signal—these boys had found me in the animal pound, and there I had faced them.

I glared at them accusingly, and taunted them. I spat at their feet.

"Yesterday," I cried, "you laughed gleefully at my discomfort when the Mullah beat me. Would any like to laugh now—any one, or two, or three?"

They remained silent. They were shamefaced.

"You are all afraid of the old man," I flung at them. "Only Bacha has enough bravery to thwart him."

They shifted uneasily on their bare feet, and eyed me askance.

Jamal Gul it was who spoke up.

"We are not afraid of the Mullah," he retorted angrily. "Perhaps it is that we require a leader. Who is there that would incur the Holy one's wrath —especially when he carries the tale to the Elders and to our fathers . . .?"

"Bacha!" they cried with one accord.

I pretended to be diffident, and I mocked them.

"Pshaw!" . . . The monosyllable was crushing and derisive. . . . "You would not follow. . . ."

"We will . . . we will. . . ."

"Follow then," I returned, hitting while the iron was hot. "Follow then to the Mullah's house. We will make him weep with vexation. We will tear down his vines."

So easily were my playmates gulled. So easily were they inveigled into what all believed to be a mere schoolboy's prank. But, of what use to me were the Mullah's vines? What satisfaction would there be in trampling them to the dust?

No, Bacha wanted more than that, and he was determined to exact vengeance. For three moons he had had in his possession a Ferenghi box containing three matches, and these now reposed in the folds of his pyjamas.

"Come," I shouted, and we left the pound at a run, and raced up the village street.

Mine was the hand that grabbed the first handful of vine, and that was all that was necessary. Other hands, once shown the initiative, carried on the work, and soon all was a scene of desolation.

One boy I called on one side.

"Unloose the Mullah's donkey," I ordered, "and ride it away into the hills and lose it."

And to another,

"Take the Mullah's horse, loosen a shoe, insert a pebble, and lame it."

In the scrimmage that proceeded, it was an easy thing to extract the matches that I had hoarded to such good purpose, and to apply one to the dry thatch of the Mullah's abode. It flared up like salt-petred tinder, enveloped the roof with a rush and a roar, and in a few moments left the four walls open to the sky.

I had had my revenge.

The others, dismayed by the unexpected, gazed at the scene, their eyes wide with perturbation. Then, all except one, Jamal, turned and fled.

I laughed.

From the shelter of a friendly tree, I surveyed the village square. I could see my father, with the *mussack* over his back, sprinkling water on the pathways in order that the Faithful might make their way decorously to the mosque. The men were on their way to pray, and as they passed, they nodded their heads dolorously in the direction of the skeleton of the Mullah's house.

"There is that good man, the water-carrier," they remarked, "making the way clean for the feet of the Faithful. Ah, but his son . . . !"

After the prayers, there were more perambulations, and that which was in the nature of a mass meeting.

Still in my tree, I could hear the Elders discussing me, and demanding that something be done to curb the rebellious spirits of one who knew not his place, being but a water-carrier's son.

One patriarch with lascivious eye, who had ever beheld me with disdain and abhorrence, led the spate of feeling against me.

"The Holy Mullah's abode has been defiled," he declaimed, "and this Bacha should be whipped and put to the meanest tasks."

A peach, over-ripe, caught the Patriarchal one on the side of the face, and the juicy liquid drooled disgustingly down his beard.

He swung round in horror and rage, intent upon discovering who it was had put such shame upon an Elder, but none in the group had seen anything untoward.

In the darkened doorway of a nearby house I could see the twitching face of Jamal. He had sense. He shouted, and created a diversion. In two seconds I was out of the tree, and on the outskirts of the village.

That night, as I lay out in the darkness, not daring to return to the village, the jackal cry, thrice repeated, brought Jamal to me. He carried a jhapati, which I ate ravenously, and a message.

It seemed that Nur Khan, the horseman I had seen upon the hillside the previous afternoon, and who, to a degree was responsible for my present plight, would have word with me.

I was suspicious, and told Jamal of my fears, but for answer he brought a knife from the folds of his shirt, and handed it to me.

"Nur Khan," he said with spirit, "would not kill a boy, but—well is he who is prepared."

I fingered the weapon lovingly, and thought of the Mullah, for it was cold upon the hillside.

"When would he speak?" I asked with more confidence.

"To-morrow," replied Jamal, and was gone.

Next day, the jackals were busy upon the hillsides, and eventually I threw a stone. It weighed several pounds, and it fell within six inches of Nur Khan's head. It was no mis-aim, and Nur Khan, who had seen Bacha at play, knew exactly what that bouncing missile portended.

He rose to his feet, and held out both hands.

"I come in peace," he cried, but there was an angry tremor behind his words, for though he knew that I was near, he had failed to locate me.

"Put down your pistol, Nur Khan," I rallied, "and also your knife. You are over-armed for a man of peace."

Sullenly, he divested himself of his weapons, placed them upon a rock, and walked forward. I emerged from my hiding-place.

Nur Khan eyed me without favour, for no Kohistan highlander likes to temporise with a boy, and he was angry.

"Are you fool, or knave?" he demanded churlishly. "Think that Nur Khan would do you hurt?"

"Many things happen upon the hillside," I replied pertly, and took care to keep my distance.

There was silence while we eyed each other, Nur Khan weighing up my physique and natural dare-devilry, and I wondering why I should have been singled out for this unconventional assignation.

The man, now that he was there, knew not how to begin, and he was patently uneasy. Sensing this, I laughed.

"Well, who are we going to rob?" I thrust the question at him, and he too laughed in his turn.

Suddenly, he ceased to be amused, and his set features betokened decision. When he spoke, he spoke earnestly, and as one to whom words come haltingly, and only after they have been well weighed.

"Let us talk in peace," he said severely. "We can be of use to each other."

Then it was that he unfolded his plan. Briefly, he schemed to rob the village Hindu money-lender, and to make his way southward. The task, as we both knew, was no easy one, for the Hindu was cunning and canny, and it was his boast that he had never lost so much as a pie's worth of jewellery. In his task, Nur Khan required assistance, and moreover, the assistance of one well-versed in the ways of the village and who would be prepared to leave it, and seek pastures anew. I, he assured me, seemed fitted for the task, both because I knew the village and would find it inconvenient to return, but also because I had displayed courage and daring which might now be put to profitable account.

When he had finished, I flashed one question at him.

"Is this to be robbery, or murder?" I demanded.

Nur Khan took a pull at his beard before replying, and I knew that I was being weighed in the balance.

"For myself," he said at length, "I know not, for my part will be to interview the Hindu. If he is wise, then it will be robbery. If he is not——!" He opened his hands in an expressive gesture.

To cut a long story short, we robbed the man; and with it sealed my partnership with Nur.

CHAPTER II

KABUL

"Who comes?" It was the ever wakeful watchman as we made our way through the village square.

In my excitement I had forgotten the existence of the village incompetent, and so, for that matter, had Nur Khan. The latter cursed.

"It is Bacha, O Watchman," I cried, "merely returned for a little food, and now on his way to the barren hillside, for the village will have none of him."

Whispering hoarsely, I beseeched Nur Khan to keep to the shadows.

"Think that I will open the gate for you?" The watchman was heavily ironic.

"No, O Watchman—I go to scale the wall—I would not get you into trouble."

"Praise be to Allah there is none other as you. Otherwise—this place would be peopled by devils." The watchman continued on his rounds, grumbling

Still fearful of discovery, and apprehensive lest the watchman's slow wits should revolve to that degree where he would wish to see the departure of the young ingrate, Bacha, Nur Khan and I mounted the wall, and in a few seconds were crouching by the house.

Nur Khan, with a heavy bundle in his hands, leaped into the saddle, and I, without waiting for an invitation, scrambled up behind. I heard Nur Khan grunt as my hands sought his waistband, and it gave me pause. Nevertheless, we went away like the wind, and when the grey light of the morning came to give shape to the countryside, we were many khosts southward of our highland village.

We spoke little during this eerie journey except when, on two occasions, Nur Khan suggested that we should change positions, and that he should take his turn in sitting behind.

The first time Nur Khan put forward the suggestion on the plea of my personal comfort. On the second, it was to ease the burden of the horse.

On each occasion there was something in his tone which made me demur. I said little, and merely grunted my replies, my tone suggesting to the man before me that I was too fatigued either to dismount or to formulate coherent responses.

Indeed, I had reason to be suspicious, and to prefer this man before me rather than behind, for so far he had said nothing in respect to the happenings in the goldsmith's room, and nothing at all about the division of that which he carried with such care in his lap.

With the dawn, Nur Khan gazed anxiously and oft over his shoulder, and frequently halted his horse in order that he might listen the more intently.

"Think that we shall be followed?" I put the question tentatively, and entirely without guile, but Nur Khan seemed to find little solace in the query.

He shrugged his massive shoulders, and peering over his bandolier strappings, vouchsafed me a queer look.

"You hang on like a leech, Bacha," was his terse comment, and he shook the horse into quicker motion.

"But"—I returned to the attack—"think you that they will organise a pursuit?" I would goad this fellow into speech, and make him speak of the loot which we must presently divide.

"When they find that we have the goldsmith's box, then they will follow—for gain!" Nur Khan at least, had no illusions about the moral outlook of his fellow villagers.

"When they find out! Won't the goldsmith raise the alarm?"

"In Gehenna, perhaps, but not in the village."

"Ah—so he is dead?"

"Yes—there was no other way. . . ."

Again he peered over his shoulder, and for the first time saw the blood-stained wrappings round my throat, and the deeply-lined gashes down my face. He grinned.

"The lady—she was not hospitable? . . . I heard the tamasha in the other room. . . . A vixen, eh?"

"She—she was terrible." My youthful spirits sank as that scene came back to me.

"A sad experience," he remarked with mocking commiseration. "But you should not be so despondent. You will not find all of them so anxious to remain unsullied."

I refused to join in the man's raillery, and dropped into silence.

Presently, at a stream, Nur Khan halted, and indeed it was time, for I had suffered agonies during that ride, and was near spent. The wound in my throat gave me great trouble, and was but poorly bandaged.

Observing my plight, Nur Khan would have me sleep.

"You must rest," he said. "Afterwards, we will proceed."

To all such behests, however, I remained obstinate, my eyes continually seeking that which my companion guarded with such care. So far, not one word had he uttered regarding the share which I had so ingloriously earned.

At length, unable to restrain my patience further, I looked pointedly at his bundle.

"How much do you think we have there?" I asked. Purposely, I stressed the collective "we."

"Who can tell," he replied airily. "This is not the time and place to play the bunia."

He eyed me curiously as I leaned against a boulder, but purely by chance my fingers were playing with a piece of rock. He hesitated, then jumped to his feet.

"Come," he said brusquely, "we have tarried enough. We cannot afford to take chances, for there are those who would rob us of our gains."

Again he besought me to take the saddle, but again I demurred, maintaining that it was better for both that the lighter weight should be behind rather than on the animal's withers. Ill-humouredly, he allowed me to have my way.

Nur Khan now proceeded with greater caution,

and his manner, when he sought out his way through the hills, was studied and deliberate. Never once did we show up against the sky-line, and never once did we pass within proximity of a village. When not studying the terrain before, my vis-à-vis had his eyes behind.

More than once he shaded his eyes with his hand, and I knew that he was troubled.

"Think that we are followed, Bacha?"

Twice, thrice, he put the question to me, but I did no more than shrug my shoulders. I had seen what he had seen, and more, but it was not for Bacha to open the eyes of Nur Khan.

For three more hours we cantered on our way, our mount by this time displaying most obvious signs of fatigue. Frequently, Nur Khan growled in his throat, and—the sound gave me little pleasure.

At length, when following the spur of a hill, he halted, and for ten long seconds spied out the land behind us. Seated there, I saw him start, and there was conviction in his tones when he said:

"They are there, Bacha. . . . That is the third time I have seen that horse. . . ."

Suddenly, his voice absorbed a different timbre, and he gazed round at me suspiciously, a surprised light dawning in his eyes.

"Bacha," he demanded, "what happened to that woman?"

"We fought," I said, sullenly.

"And . . . ?"

"You can see my clothes. You can see where she scratched my face, and then—when you called— I came."

Nur Khan twisted in his saddle, and the twitching muscles of his face were awry with anger and perturbation.

"Son of a low-born," he shrieked, "you have killed a woman!"

So this was to be the manner of the quarrel. This was to be the excuse for jettisoning me by the wayside—the excuse for which Nur Khan had cudgelled his brains ever since he had that bundle safely in his hands. From the very outset of our ride I knew that my companion had not the slightest intention of dividing his spoil with a boy, and now the moment had come.

"You strangled her," he bellowed. "Else—why all those deep scratches down your face? The woman did that as you throttled her, you low-born. Is it remarkable that we are followed?" He spat, and twisted further in his seat, his near-side stirrup leather taut, and nearly horizontal.

He snarled, and spat in my face.

"Off you go, you spawn of a camel," he mouthed, and would have struck me a blow in the face which would have sent me hurtling down the khudside. But, with hand uplifted, he paused, and his eyes, as they gazed into mine, saw the death which he had been so assiduously wooing.

I, too, spat, and his arm remained in the air.

"Would rob and kill a boy, would you?" My words were heavy with satire, and I laughed leeringly, back into those thunderstruck eyes.

Nur Khan could feel my knife in his back in a spot which I had selected after hours of silent and amusing contemplation. It pierced the skin just over his kidney, and it sank deeper. Then, with a thrust, and a wrench, the steel was buried to the hilt, and was playing merry with his skewered intestines.

Slowly, that uplifted arm fell; slowly those eyes, but a few inches from mine, lost their brightness, and became tired, and filmed. Slowly, Nur Khan toppled sideways, fell to the narrow mountain path, rolled to the edge, and disappeared in the abyss below—food for the jackals.

Once, twice, thrice, I emulated the call of those to whom I had presented a feast, and faintly the answer came.

Shortly, I could discern the outline of the Mullah's pony, and then the cheery countenance of Jamal.

Nur Khan was right—we had been followed!

For three further days and nights Jamal and I traversed the passes, keeping well away from habitation, and existing on the small amount of food which Jamal had brought with him.

Once, we opened Nur Khan's bundle, and feasted our eyes on the golden trinkets which it contained— anklets for the feet, bangles for the arm and stars and rings for the nose. We dreamed of the day when we would sell our treasure, and be rich.

On the morning of the fourth day, we had our first sight of Kabul, and long was the discussion during which we evolved and demolished a dozen plans.

Finally, we resolved to tell something which approximated to the truth, and at least had the merit of sounding feasible and plausible. We were two lads from the northern highlands come south to seek our fortunes. With us were two horses which we might, or might not be disposed to sell, and a quantity of jewellery, the property of my late and very revered mother.

We had no difficulty in locating the caravanserai, where we tethered our horses and left them in the charge of a chowkidar. Then, with our bundle jealously guarded, we made our way to the bazaars, and to the street of goldsmiths.

Never shall I forget the pucker of amusement which hid the black, beady eyes of the merchant to whom we displayed our wealth.

"Indeed," he said facetiously, "your mother was a rich and honoured woman. Your father lavished his rupees upon her!"

"Yes," I dubiously agreed.

The man turned to me.

"You say that your name is Bacha Saquo . . . I say that you are the son of a rascal."

He touched the trinkets disdainfully with the tip of his finger.

"Gold!" And he rolled backwards, and laughed.

"But one is of gold, my striplings," he gurgled, "and the others are of base metal, sheeted with the precious covering."

Jamal and I eyed each other dismayed. Deep down in my throat I cursed Nur Khan for the fool that he was, for even in death the goldsmith had got the better of the bargain.

"How much?" I asked hesitantly, my aplomb having deserted me and all thoughts of immediate riches soaring away in the smoke from this man's hookah.

The merchant eyed me appraisingly.

"Thirty rupees," he answered. He sighed lugubri-
ously, and by his manner he conveyed the impression
that he was robbing himself.

"Thirty!" There was both horror and anger in
my tone. "Come," I added, confidently, and
wheedlingly, "surely you jest, hadji. You mean
a hundred?"

The man lost interest, and listlessly scooped the
trinkets together, and pushed them towards me.

"Eighty," I broke in anxiously.

He pulled gurglingly at his hookah, and we might
not have been there.

"Sixty?"

Slowly, the merchant returned to life, and once
more his eyes fell to the trinkets.

"Thirty-two," he said with a great air of finality,
"and—I go hungry."

"Thirty-five," I countered desperately.

The man put out his talons, picked up the poor
pieces of finery, and tossed them into a nearby
bowl. He was both bored and sleepy.

"Thirty-three," he answered, pulling out a small
sack, and thirty-three it was.

Nearly twenty of our rupees Jamal and I spent
on fine raiment. I secured voluminous and faultless
Pathan trousers, a white tunic caught in at the
waist by an embroidered belt, and over my tunic
that which indeed indicated man's estate—an ornate,
and beautifully worked waistcoat. My turban was
of dark blue material, set around a gold-embroidered
kullah. Jamal looked very much the same, except
that his trousers were perhaps not quite so voluminous, his tunic lacked the embroidered waistline, his

waistcoat was plain and his turban was rolled around a kullah of khaki.

Well pleased with ourselves in our finery, and still with rupees retained in our waistbands, we repaired to the caravanserai where we sought out the chowkidar.

He raised his stick in salutation when he saw us, and his manner was servile. His old eyes gave forth of their admiration.

"You men from the north know how to strike a hard bargain!" He grinned, knowingly, and I, well-pleased to have been called a man, grinned back.

"Two hundred and fifty rupees for those two sorry crocks!" He laughed uproariously, and slapped his thighs.

"Stay!" I regarded the man with little favour.

"Stay!" I repeated. "What old crocks? . . . What two hundred and fifty rupees?"

The poor fool drooped an eyelid, and tittered at what he was pleased to imagine a pleasantry.

"Your horses—bahadur—those which you sold in the bazaar. You must have told a handsome tale, for the man seemed well pleased with his bargain."

"Bargain?"

"Well—he seemed to think so. He showed me the receipt, and described both you and the horses. There could be no mistake, so I allowed him to take them away . . .!"

For more than three years Jamal and I tarried in the Afghan capital, working with the horse-thieves from the mountains, and those who came to Kabul to dispose of the loot of caravans. We fed well, and we dressed well, for we soon learned the dark, hidden ways of the bazaar, and we could be of the greatest assistance to those who came from the hills and knew not the ways of the townsmen. Even so, we had to exercise care, for these were the days of the Ameer Habibullah, and the way of transgressors could be both irksome and gory. Moreover, there was an innate suspicion of those who came from Kohistan—a suspicion which even our carefully-fostered ingenuousness could not entirely dispel.

It was not that such a halcyon existence could continue, and our departure from Kabul was both swift, and unpremeditated.

An officer of the royal bodyguard barred our progress one night, and he was a swashbuckler. He suggested that the horse we were leading came from the Royal stables, but the man lied. It belonged to a wealthy merchant on the outskirts of the city, and it had just been clipped and dyed so that not even its real owner would have recognised it.

The man, however, was persistent, and rude withal. He drew his sword, and called lustily for the guard which, of course, was unfortunate. And, for an officer of the Royal bodyguard, the man did little with his opportunities, for his wallet yielded but twelve Kabuli rupees.

Thereafter, the capital was unsafe, for the Ameer frowned upon those who disembowelled his liveried retainers.

Three months later we were slipping through the Khyber, and for the first time I viewed the land of

Hindustan and the Ferenghi in his own habitat.
The English, by the way, even though they be
Infidel, can laugh like men. They laugh with their
stomachs, and not with their eyes as do the Hindu.
Their humour is as ours, and is not caustic and
acrimonious. Yet, many of their jokes I could
never understand, even though I was aware that
there was humour, and not merely taunting vindic-
tiveness. Yes, I liked the Ferenghi, because he
could laugh at simple things, and could appreciate
a horse, and a dog, and bravery—even when that
was directed against himself. But—it intrigued me
for long, and not any of the scribes of the bazaar
could translate the idiom. Thirty miles to the westward of Peshawar is Kohat—a fine city to the
unsophisticated eyes of an hillman, but a miserable,
mud-walled pestilence when one has beheld cities
such as Peshawar. There, in Kohat, there was the
the magistrate—the deputy commissioner—and as
Jamal pointed out, on the board outside his residence
was his name; . . . well . . . I would not give it
here!

Now a magistrate—and a deputy commissioner
—is a man of power and of substance, even among
his own, yet the officers and others of the class
never referred to him as "Bara Sahib."

Always was it: "old man", even to his face, and
while the men would laugh and enjoy the quip—
for a joke there must have been—the women within
earshot would purse their lips, talk the more ani-
matedly, and pretend not to have heard.

Peshawar, the city of roses and chrysanthemums,
the fine civil station with its polo-playing officers

and its tea-drinking memsahibs, and the colourful, kaleidoscopic bazaar, where in the course of one single day, one can meet men of all classes and of all countries. Peshawar—with its seething city within, and its calm, peaceful, almost somnolent civil station without, where even though they be on the Frontier line, and right in the mouth of the Khyber, the white men play their games and then repair to their club to make merry.

How many have been deceived by this? How many have failed to see below the surface?

How many have been gulled by this seeming foolishness of the Ferenghi—a Ferenghi which, with perfect equanimity hear the bazaar laughing in its hand because the postmaster of the city was an Afghan. What childishness! What suckling innocence! Yet, was it foolishness? What matter what happened in the post office at Peshawar when every telegraphist across the border with his miserable eight rupees per month was in the pay of these softly-spoken white men whom one never saw in uniform!

I speedily made a discovery. The battalions of armed constabulary who did duty in the city were not those who really maintained order. The sentries who prowled around the civil station and did duty over the armouries were not really those who enabled the officers to play their polo and their tennis and to dance at their club.

No, behind the parade, there were others—quiet, retiring individuals of amazing knowledge.

There was one—Brickman, or so I shall call him, —who sat in his bungalow, outwardly the most uninspiring of men. His most prized possession, so his Pathan orderly told me, was an enormous brass bedstead which took to pieces, and which he had imported from vilayet. 'Twas said that it was a gift from his aunt.

When the Bolsheviki over-ran Russia to the Oxus, and even swamped the Emirate of Bokhara, all sorts and conditions of refugees made their painful way through Afghanistan, to emerge, with feelings of tremendous relief, from the mouth of the Khyber at the fort of Jamrud. Here, civilians would interrogate them, and by devious paths they would find their way to this bungalow in the civil station. There, Brickman would interview them in every language; in every patois. No man—or woman—could get by on the score of being misunderstood, and many there were who were caught in this nearly invisible net.

Tolerant, lackadaisical English! How they scheme behind those easy, gentlemanly manners which fit them like a glove!

Bacha Saquo, though he could not learn of the Mullah, could of the English, so—he sold tea—a pleasing, profitable pastime which shrouded a multitude of activities which would have caused this Sahib to leap from his bedstead in chagrin had he the veriest inkling of them.

Many a ·303 rifle bolt was filched from the barracks under the very eyes of the soldiery; many a polo pony disappeared, to make its way across the Indus, through the ravine country around Attock, and southward to Rawalpindi, to be sold in the marts of Lahore, Murree, Sialkot, Amritsar and elsewhere.

Yes, tea proved a profitable pastime, and I, Bacha, thought of marriage.

There was one in the bazaar to whom I boasted. Bacha Saquo was no water-carrier's son, but the heir of a rich landowner in Kohistan—hence, his fine raiment. And the merchant would finger the texture, listen to my stories of our fine house, and his eyes would glisten.

One day he made a proposition.

Would I like to be his son-in-law?

I was polite, but not enamoured.

Why should I have been? Was not I the only son of a landowner, and rich withal, and was this man but a merchant.

But, with tears in his eyes, he persisted, and spoke of the dowry. He spoke oft of the dowry, and at length I capitulated.

Yet, the man drove a hard bargain even in his marriage settlements, for his daughter was ugly to look upon, and she had vinegar in her veins instead of warm, red blood.

A harridan, several years my senior, she made life exceedingly irksome for a tea merchant, and the other side of my business received increasing attention. This woman, through ways of her own, took not long to discover that I was not a rich landowner's son, and openly taunted me with living on her bounty. She was a she cat, immense, and gross.

So it was that I was often abroad, chance frequently taking me across the border, ostensibly to meet the caravans, but actually to dispose of rifle bolts, and occasionally a complete rifle.

And this vixenish jade, stuffing herself with sweetmeats in Peshawar, very nearly encompassed my death.

The chief of one Khyber village made himself especially hospitable, and I called him friend. Often we had business to discuss, for he would take my bolts and rifles and transport them further into the hinterland in the knowledge that each further mile from the Frontier increased their value. It was a pleasing combination, and we worked in harmony.

Ultimately I became his son-in-law; and taking advantage of the chief's absence the rival clans launched a tribal attack during which many men were slain. Also women took a hand in it, against women of other clans, and my wife, as a result thereof, died of fatal injuries. Hearing of this I hurried to the scene, but it was too late.

CHAPTER III

THE AMULET

THE gossip of the Frontier travels fast, and as I wended my way through the Khyber as a peaceful merchant attached to a small caravan, fuller report of the debacle of my home reached me. The Ferenghi police, with their usual perspicacity, speedily discarded any thought of murder, and rightly, they attributed the deaths to an exuberant outburst of tribal passion. They need not have wondered why the tea seller thought it expedient so expeditiously to depart, with his knife in his teeth.

It behoved me, however, to move with considerable circumspection through the tribal tracts, because the chief, my bride's father, would have had word of her unseemly demise, and his view of the occurrence might not have been so charitable. Later, I thought, rather than to start an inter-clan war of revenge, it was best to terminate the sorry story; and leave the region.

Frankly, I knew not where to wend my steps. I had had no news from Kabul, and to show my face there might well provoke trouble. Where court darlings are concerned, Eastern officials are apt to have long memories, and—I had never been able to ascertain whether I had been connected with the removal of that bumptious swordsman of the Royal bodyguard.

Equally, it would be unwise to direct my steps

to Kohistan where the death of the goldsmith and
his wife would still be vividly remembered and a
subject for nightly discussion round the village fires.

Actually, now that I knew that the Peshawar
police did not associate me with murder, I had
serious thoughts of returning to Hindustan, and
making my abode in Rawalpindi, or even Lahore.
Both cities, I was certain, would provide ample
scope for one of my temperament.

It was while in this state of mental indecision
that I fell in with a Mullah. He was a worthy
man, and when he made his way to our encampment one evening, we gave him salutation.

He was a Holy man, and one of wide travel,
and because of his holiness it was that he saw the
cynic that was within me.

He sought me out, and squatted on the edge of
my bedding roll, and looked into my eyes by the
light of the moon. It was a piercing, yet impersonal
stare, and I could not take umbrage.

"I see," he said solemnly, "the mark of death."

He held up a hand to silence the laughter which
welled within me, and chided:

"You are young, but—already you have killed!"

"What would you?" I retorted. "It was my
life, or another's."

Again he peered into my eyes, and he laid his
hand gently on my arm.

"I see you rising," he continued. "Rising . . .
rising to a high estate upon the bodies of the fallen.
There is blood . . . there is ribald laughter . . .
there is lamentation."

"I am to be a brigand?" I was openly facetious.

Again he held up his hand, and again allowed it softly to rest on my arm.

He gazed up at the moon, and was lost in meditation.

"There will be many kings," he said at length. "There will be six or seven—I cannot see clearly, but eventually you, young man, will assume the Royal raiment. . . ."

I laughed within myself. Here, at least was news, and good news, for if this Mullah were not entirely *be-akul* it would mean that my span of life would be generous.

The life of kings—six or seven, he had said.

True, ugly rumours were on every lip in Afghanistan. There were those who said, over boldly, that the Ameer had made a bad bargain with the Russians in the matter of the Oxus, and that in failing to obtain the ancient provinces of Shignan and Roshan, and in failing to extricate himself from the dominance of the British, now miserably weakened by their long wars overseas, he had fallen between two stools, and had served his country badly.

The people said that the Ameer was gorged with British gold, and was selling his birthright, and that of the nation.

The life of kings . . . it was an intriguing thought.

Already, in the political agitation which was sweeping Afghanistan, there had been an ugly indication of popular temper. Only a few months previously, so word had come to Peshawar, a bullet had been aimed at the Ameer as he drove through the chirag-lit streets of the Chore bazaar. No Bacha Saquo had been behind that trigger, for the bullet had missed. Even so——

My gaze returned to the Mullah, and though he smiled at me there was sadness in his eyes.

He fumbled in his garments, and bade me loosen my sleeve. Wonderingly, I did so, and he bared my arm. To my bare flesh he attached an amulet.

"Young man," he said rising, and giving me salutation, "despise not what I have given thee. It will charm away the bullets, and divert the assassin's knife. Its potency will remain with thee as long as I remain upon this earth, and . . . for two moons beyond."

He was gone, swallowed up in the darkness.

For as long as the Mullah lived, and—for two moons.

Could there be anything in what the man had said? It seemed improbable, and this latter computation of my life's span was not so comforting.

For as long as he lived . . . and for two moons. . . .

Yet, the Mullah was already aged, and even Holy men do not live for ever.

Still, there was this matter of kings—that, at least promised much that warmed my heart. . . .

Yet, before the morn, I was to think deeply on the words of the Mullah.

Even as he addressed me, one king was dead, and another was both in the making, and in the decline.

Two kings were to depart before the sun set again on the barren rocks of the tribal lands. And, I had scoffed!

Even as the Mullah spoke, Ameer Habibullah was encamped in the Kullah Ghos Pass, in Lughman Province. He had been hunting, and was fatigued, and—he slept. It was his last sleep, for an assassin crept into his bed-chamber, and shot him through the temple with a revolver. This was on the night of February 19, 1919.

Next morning, the drums had rolled the news to every corner of Afghanistan, and we in the caravan knew that the ruler was dead, if not the manner of his passing.

As the sun rolled high in the heavens, the roll of the drums could be heard again, and there were those who could augment their information by word of mouth.

The dead king's younger brother, Sirdar Nasrullah Khan, then at Jalalabad, had proclaimed himself Ameer.

This was quick work, but others were quicker in this wild scramble for a throne, and before the sun had passed its meridian we had other news news from the northward.

Amanullah Khan, the dead Ameer's third son, was Governor of Kabul.

Sirdar Inayatullah Khan, the first son, and the heir, had waived his rights to the throne when his uncle at Jalalabad had rushed to the forefront. The second son, and the next in succession, Sirdar Hidayatullah Khan experienced one of those minor, yet exceedingly unfortunate mishaps that can change the whole trend of a man's life.

On the night that his father was murdered, and even while I was in converse with the Mullah, he had been motoring to Kabul to relieve Amanullah Khan of the Governorship. His motor (this was 1919) broke down, and he was stranded.

And, Amanullah Khan was in the capital!

Amanullah acted, even though his uncle had forestalled him at Jalalabad.

He called out the troops, and held a monster parade.

He told the men of his father's death, and he wept, copiously.

"And, what of my uncle?" he cried. "Is he acting in accord with true Afghan traditions?

"Has he not proclaimed himself king, even before the murderer of my beloved father has been found and tried?"

He sobbed, and drew his sword.

"Never," he exclaimed through his tears, "will I sheath my sword until the murderer of my father has been brought to book, I—who am but the slave of the nation."

That last declamation made Amanullah King.

There was a wild shout, and rifles and talwars were raised in the air. Like one man, the soldiers chanted:

"Thy father was our benefactor. . . . Thy honour is our honour, our beloved Prince. . . . You are now our King."

In such manner are thrones emptied and re-occupied.

When we heard the news, I laughed in my hand, for I knew that the people of Kohistan, and many in the Frontier tribal tracts, would regard Amanullah as an interloper. Even so, rumour said, there were those in Kabul who failed to see in Amanullah the rightful heir, because, as third son, at no time had he been regarded as the probable successor to his father.

Yet, there were greybeards who said that the new king would do well. He was no mere princeling, they said. Had he not been entrusted with affairs of state, and had he not been Governor of Kabul?

But, I, who had been in the capital, and behind the scenes, saw trouble looming in the distance. Like many another man, he was afflicted of his in-laws, and I had seen what I had seen.

Again I bethought of the Mullah, and of his extraordinary words.

I could see trouble . . . death . . . blood . . . much as he had painted it.

But Amanullah was well versed in the ways of state, and his span was to be lengthy. In many ways he had sound common sense, and who can fail to applaud his first action?

He increased the pay of the soldiery to twenty rupees per month. That settled the army.

He promised the country as a whole, an unqualified national freedom, entirely divorced from British interference. That settled the agitators.

That accomplished, he proceeded to deal with possible rivals.

Word came over the passes that there had been arrests in Jalalabad. Sirdar Nasrullah Khan, who had proclaimed himself ruler so precipitately, and Amanullah's elder brother, Sirdar Inayatullah Khan, who had acquiesced to the arrangement, found themselves surrounded by soldiers and bayonets. They were taken to Kabul, and placed under strict surveillance, together with Mohamed Nadir Khan. (The Afghan Commander-in-Chief who was eventually to oust Bacha Saquo from Kabul.)

A number of officers of the Jalalabad garrison were tried and executed for their part in the naming of Sirdar Nasrullah Khan as King, and—the Sirdar died in prison.

Both Amanullah's brother, and Mohamed Nadir Khan, however, were released.

Thus it was, while masquerading as a peaceful merchant, that I saw the hand of Fate strike with lightning rapidity at my country. Each day brought fresh news, and each man his fresh crop of rumours.

Then, also, the words of the Mullah were strangely unsettling. There was unrest everywhere—in Afghanistan, on the border, in Hindustan itself, beyond the northern borders in Russia, and over the seas where mighty nations had been locked in mortal combat.

The most amazing stories were told of the fighting beyond the waters, and many said that the might of the British raj had dimmed and that shortly would return the days when profitable descents upon the Indus and beyond might be contemplated.

This was the opportunity to rise—rise.

Should I, or should I not, gamble with my destiny?

For days I contemplated the issue, and in time came to Jalalabad, still quite undecided whether I should repair to Kabul, return to Kohistan and seek my fortunes amidst the tribesmen of mine own hills, return to Hindustan, or just vegetate.

No, Bacha, could never do the latter.

In my distress of mind, I began to frequent the bazaars and to gamble.

My stock of rupees increased, and increased, until I had to take special precautions to guard my wealth, for one cannot win money by such means without others knowing the extent of one's gains.

Still, I could not make up my mind, and still I gambled. Then, slowly, but yet with many little heartening spurts in the right direction, my luck changed. Instead of heaping silver into my money bags, I found that I was pouring it out. Still, I reflected, this could be but a temporary phase, and one which every gambler must face.

But, the ill-fortune was not temporary. It persisted, and the more I strove to replenish my hoard, the lighter it became.

There came the night when I threw my last rupee on the dice, and then followed the carpets, and the expensive silks which I had brought with me from Peshawar.

The silks saved me, and I went to my quarters that night still with rupees to jingle. But, the next night saw the end. There came the throw when I finally and irrevocably lost.

For one hot, blinding minute, I essayed to throw my embroidered waistcoat in the face of Fate, but wisely I desisted. No true-born Afghan descends to such depths.

Nevertheless, I was pice-less, and in what was tantamount to a strange country.

What was there for me to do?

I thought of the new King, and his promise of twenty rupees per month.

I enlisted.

CHAPTER IV

A SOLDIER OF THE KING

On February 28, 1919, the day that Amanullah officially became King, I adopted his uniform, and became eligible for his bounty. Primarily, I admit, the thought of the twenty rupees per month drew me to his standard, but in the short interim which there was between his declaration to his army in Kabul and his official assumption of the throne, there was his decree of unqualified national freedom.

This declaration inspired and enthralled me, the more so as it quickly became evident that the Ferenghi way back of the Durand Line were doing some hard thinking.

I enlisted, was given a rifle which was a joy— a thing of balance and of wonderful precision— adequate rations, and the promise of pay.

I, Bacha Saquo, who had killed his man, and knew more of hill warfare than the bucolic officers who were commissioned to teach us the ways of modern armies, was placed in the awkward squad. The relegation hurt, more especially as he whose arm was decorated with the all-important chevrons had a caustic tongue, and an eye for trivialities, and military niceties which were aggravating to one of my spirit.

Yet, I have to confess with chagrin, I made a profound discovery. Until I was ushered forth on to that barrack square I knew not of the mysteries of right or left.

That one could win battles by stepping off with the left foot foremost, seemed to me incredible, yet seemingly it was so. Also, it seemed to my hill-man's mind that to remain shoulder to shoulder, with men left and right, left remarkably little room for the passage of the enemy's bullets. But, I was assured it was not so—that the drill kitab said it was demanded, and that the Ferenghis invariably adopted this practice.

I admit that I made a poor parade ground soldier; that the cant of my rifle was never such as the others'; that my step was ever wrong leg foremost, and that the puttees with which I was required to bind my calves were a snare and an abomination.

Nevertheless, there were moments when I could laugh in my sleeve at the vituperative drill-officer, who was my squad commander.

On the parade ground, he would hold forth loud and long on the technique of the modern rifle. Admittedly, it was wonderful that these weapons should not require ramrods and powder horns, but they were not as amazing as all that. Apparently, the most astonishing thing about them was their sighting—something which I could never comprehend, and artificialities which I persistently ignored. If an object was at a distance, I elevated the muzzle accordingly. Any child of the hills can do that, and—no hillman can afford to waste ammunition.

For weeks this worthy officer discoursed on parade ground manœuvres, and the intricacies of the rifle. Then he marshalled us in his stupid formation, and we went to the outskirts of the city to fire at paper targets. Immense these were, with ink-drawn rings, and a large blob in the middle which all who would consider themselves efficient must hit.

The officer soon initiated us into the routine. If one hit the target, men concealed in the ground would mark the event by waving a flag up and down—once for the outer ring, twice for the next, thrice for the next, and four times for the blob. Unthinkable, but—if one missed, the flag would be waved horizontally and derisively, to and fro.

The officer threw out his chest, and informed us that he would instruct us in the art, and would take a sighting shot. With great care, and mighty ceremonial, he secured his paunch to the earth, played with his sights, took a deep breath, held it, closed one eye, counted five before he depressed the trigger, and fired.

He rose triumphantly, and turned to us, awaiting our polite plaudits.

From the butts a flag waved horizontally, and a derisive titter broke from the ranks. Disconsolately, the officer fixed me with a wintry eye.

"That," he said grandly, searching frantically for his lost aplomb, "is to show you *rangruts* how *not* to do it."

We were suitably impressed.

Still holding me with a censorious eye, the officer bade me take my place at the firing point. His position was still desperate, and he had to make a gesture in order to restore his sense of discipline. He was out to make a dreadful example.

I fell to the earth, forgetting, in the excitement

of the moment, his carefully phrased and oft-repeated exhorts respecting position. As I fell I fired, to the rage, yet inner satisfaction of he who must bluster.

"Observe," he said with ironical emphasis, "how these wild badmashes from the hills forget the words of their mentors. Observe how this man, who would be a soldier, forgot to align his sights; how he fired wildly, like a raw woodsman blasting shot at a covey of pigeon. He thought he had a blunderbuss in his hands. He forgets that he has a rifle—an instrument of astounding accuracy, and one that has to be treated with reverence and with care."

Meanwhile the men at the targets were signalling vertically, twice, three, four times, and I was well pleased, though hardly elated, for had the object not been a stationary one? Had it been smaller, and swift of movement, there might have been cause for jubilation, but—this!

But, enough. Not for me to say that every time I fired I hit. It was not for me to be amazed or incredulous—that part was reserved for the officer. I should have been ashamed and disgusted had I done otherwise, for it was but child's play for one of my upbringing.

Briefly, I became the crack shot of the newly-joined in Amanullah's army, and as time proceeded, and further comparisons could be made, easily the most assured marksman amongst all who bore his uniform.

During the time that I, with so many others, was required to perform senseless evolutions at the barkings of parade ground instructors, Amanullah was already in the throes of his first war. He had to uphold his word, that he would give his country complete freedom by the force of arms.

Ordinarily, of course, he would have hesitated in the course which he adopted, but in truth he was committed before he was officially recognised as King, due to the pressure of the Afghan public opinion to wrestle for national freedom. Unless the British were prepared to adopt a certain course, that first declaration to his peoples spelled war at the outset. And, the British, they said, were not disposed to take this course. Indeed, they were exceedingly chary in accepting Amanullah as the rightful ruler. While drilling on the barrack square I had much to occupy my mind for, in the ways of war, there is little that is hidden from the people of Afghanistan.

This much I have to say for Amanullah—I do not believe that he deliberately dragged his coat. I believe that he entered upon hostilities with Great Britain, if with some perturbation, at least not without enthusiasm. He was a King who had to make a gesture of power—one who was forced by political expediency to force the issue of Afghanistan's independence, for which his people had clamoured for long.

Great Britain did not help him in the matter. When he sent his Note to the Viceroy, acquainting him of the death of his father and his assumption of the throne, and of his desire to come to an understanding, in a friendly spirit, on the matter of Afghanistan's independence, and other questions, he received no reply for six weeks, and then the reply evaded the issue—a sure sign in the eyes of many of his counsellors that the British Raj was determined to retain in its hands the control of Afghan foreign affairs.

Amanullah was badly counselled in most matters. I, who had spent so much time in Hindustan, could have unveiled his eyes, but I was a humble sepoy on the barrack square at Jalalabad. I was no lisping courtier. I had lived, and had peeped behind the scenes. Amanullah had lived, but there was much that he had to take at its face value.

Looking at the border situation, when rendered to paper, Amanullah saw a number of startling facts—a situation which was unlikely to recur, and which, if he were to have his way, provided him with a series of strategical circumstances which might well spell success to a sudden recourse to arms.

The vocalists were about him in full cry, and it was a pretty tale they had to unfold. According to them the whole of Hindustan was ablaze with insurrection. These men did not lie—they had only to produce the British newspapers to find corroboration for their words.

In 1919 India was a hotbed of sedition, and a maelstrom of heated, exotic, mob fever. None could tell what would happen next, and in many of the large cities the British took the precaution of removing their womenfolk to a place of comparative safety.

Straws in the wind! There were so many straws that the fields were rendered barren of corn.

From Peshawar to Bombay armed mobs, led on by revolutionaries, were tearing up railway lines, were setting fire to property, were robbing banks, pillaging the countryside.

There was fighting at Ahmedabad, Delhi, Lahore, Amritsar, Kasur, and elsewhere, and where there was not fighting, there was an undercurrent of unrest which kept troops chained to the area, and rendered much of the British army immobile.

Moreover, there was said to be considerable unrest among the troops themselves. Without a doubt all were war weary, and the British troops, fast returning to India from distant battlefields, were disgruntled. They were hungry for their homeland. The same could be said of the Indian sepoys, many of whom had not seen their lands and their relatives for four years, and were anxious, at least, for very extended leave.

Also, it was freely said that once Afghanistan put her troops into motion, the revolutionaries of Hindustan would give Amanullah every assistance.

Did they? . . . They were too busily engaged in skurrying back to their boltholes, or in hiding behind the dhoties of those whom they had induced to accept the dubious honour of the front rank of battle.

I, Bacha Saquo, could have told Amanullah that that would have happened. Life across the border was an education. I at least learned truly to appraise the value of noise, and—in Peshawar city there is that in great volume.

Amanullah Khan, because of his position, and because of the inept beings around him, cannot be wholly blamed for misreading these signs.

Even so, Amanullah did not march upon the frontier in force, with bands playing and colours flying. Rather did he press on with his *idée fixe* to that degree where war suddenly engulfed him. That at least must be the reason for the sorry dispositions which he made, for no soldier worthy of merit would have disposed his forces as he did if he believed hostilities to be imminent.

Perhaps no man living has studied this monarch as I have studied him. I know something of his whims and much of his weaknesses. I still think that he was but a big bluffer and one who, even at that very early stage, might have lost his throne if he had made one more mistake.

As it was, when Amanullah received his tardy and unsatisfactory reply from Delhi, he had to do something to save his people's face, and to indicate to the British Viceroy that there was determination behind his declaration of Afghan independence. Accordingly, he mobilised all his regular troops, and this state of military preparedness obtained for several weeks—a fact which undoubtedly excited and inflamed the never very deeply hidden war propensities of the tribesmen.

In any event, a tribal chief, who alleged that he had been directly incited by Afghan leaders, disposed of a number of coolies across the border, and soldiers of a border post strayed beyond their limits. These relatively insignificant factors applied the torch to the pyre, and soon all was roaring merrily, or—perhaps not so merrily.

Sirdar Mohamed Nadir Khan, the Commander-in-Chief, had been arrested at Jalalabad with

Amanullah's uncle and brother, and though he had
been released, he was still under a cloud. Consequently, for a time, Amanullah was his own
commander, and I, who knew nothing of parade
ground refinements and cared less, but instinctively
knew something of the art of war, trembled because of his pathetic ignorance of the elements of
strategy.

With the forces at his command, he could never
hope for a sustained success against the British, yet
he had concentrated his main host on the Khyber
where the enemy were strongest and best able to
repel any dagger thrust from across the border.

There was no finesse in this—not even an element
of Afghan stratagem. The majority of the remainder
of his arms, he directed toward Kandahar—another
ancient battleground, and then he bethought of
Sirdar Mohamed Nadir Khan. It was as well that
he did.

It was not a very nice pill for the new King to
swallow, for barely a month before he had dragged
Nadir Khan from Jalalabad in disgrace. Now he
turned to him, and, emphasising the danger to
Afghanistan's national life, appealed for his assistance. He could not offer the erstwhile Commander-
in-Chief the command.

Indeed, he had little to offer him at all, but
someone had made it clear to Amanullah that he
had left his flank up in the air and perfectly
unprotected, and in the emergency, he had to appeal
to someone who understood war. The Khost flank
had been entirely forgotten, but Amanullah raked
up a few troops and a meagre armament, and

pleaded with Nadir Khan to do his best. Gallant Nadir accepted.

It was not pleasant to go: "Left, right; left, right," under a choleric and supine drill officer while there was real war in progress, yet so it was. My view of the hostilities was not a pleasant one. Frequently, the British bombing aeroplanes appeared in the sky and bombed Jalalabad and raked the ground with machine-gun fire, and there was nothing one could do but seek the shelter of the nearest ravine. Even our wonderful officer was helpless in such a contingency, and ran to take cover with the best.

No, it was not a pleasant thought being so near to the scene of conflict and being debarred from participation. If the war had continued, and had not been extraordinarily brief, we *rangruts* would, of course, have been drafted in. As it was, all was over before we quite realised that there was peace.

It was unpleasant, also, to learn of the setbacks to Afghan arms in the nearby Khyber. The main Afghan force, with great élan, opened the war with an attack on Landi Khana on May 8th, and we lost ground. Further attacks were delivered with little success on May 16th, but on the next day it was the turn of the British. They had consolidated a large force which broke our line at the Khyber, and the British found themselves in possession of a goodly slice of Afghan territory.

The one bright spot in the campaign as far as we were concerned centred around the ill-armed force under Sirdar Mohamed Nadir Khan. Acting as a soldier should, he did not make known his plans to the enemy, and for long his line of march mystified the British.

He purposely selected country which had been reported as impassable for large bodies of troops, and suddenly appeared before the city and fort of Thal with 300 Afghan infantry, a large force of tribesmen, and seven pieces of German artillery with which he proceeded to knock great holes in the sides of the fort.

From all accounts it was pretty shooting, and when, some time later, I was in the vicinity and saw the bedraggled walls of Thal fort, I was sorry that I had not been there to see the fun. There was a good blaze too, before the place was invested by the Afghans, for the shelling set large stocks of bhoosa and petrol on fire, and one wall of the fort was entirely blackened by the blaze.

This commanding sweep by Nadir Khan robbed me of my part in the hostilities, for with Nadir Khan eating into British territory on the flank, the projected British advance on Jalalabad from the Khyber side was held up, and then the war was over.

Actually, but for the successes on the Khost and Kandahar sections, hostilities might have been over much sooner, for within ten days of the outbreak of war, the new Commander-in-Chief, Selah Mohamed Khan, after his reverses in the Khyber region, threw out suggestions of a stale mate. Nadir Khan alone saved our honour.

As it was, we Afghans were happy to emerge from the war as we did, and Amanullah's star was certainly in the ascendant, otherwise he might easily have been presented with a debacle. By the greatest stroke of good fortune, he achieved his ends, and when peace was concluded at Rawalpindi, British dominance over Afghanistan's foreign relations was removed for all time.

He did not deserve his success, for he almost went to pains to confuse the issue to his generals. The messages which he sent to the three fronts were contradictory, and at no time did the commander of one force know what was the real objective of the others.

The King's conduct in this and other respects caused me to open my eyes. When hostilities ceased, and thoughts of immediate war had receded into the distance, I was able to review in my mind the potentialities of the situation.

It all came to this:

You, Bacha Saquo, could have done much better.

The man now King at Kabul is an incompetent.

Though there is peace on paper, there is war in the air. Bacha Saquo can smell it in his nostrils.

Bacha Saquo has not forgotten the Mullah, but in the meantime, he will bide his time.

I could see trouble in the near distance.

Amanullah was weak, but he was lucky. Around him were forces which would please him and cajole him. He was afflicted of in-laws, and he was a man who must always be striking a posture.

Time could not be on the side of a man like that.

In the interim, off the barrack square, I was having an interesting army career.

CHAPTER V

I FIGHT THE REBELS

In the few years that I remained as a soldier of Amanullah, there was much to intrigue one who was looking for the sign. The Mullah must have seen the portent aright, for all over the world there were events which were gradually to produce the requisite atmosphere in which a freebooter and an opportunist might shine.

In far off America there were Indian extremists preparing to spread the cult of the revolver and the bomb in their native country. In far off Moscow there were schools in which Indian revolutionaries were being taught the difficult art of propaganda. In far off London a British Prime Minister was saying the most repugnant things about Turkey, and in Kabul, London, Delhi and Leningrad there were intrigues which had the Central Asian capitals as their focal point.

With the end of the Third Afghan War, the British Raj in India underwent a most unenviable time. The revolutionaries did their part, and the atmosphere was made all the more electric because of what victorious Foreign Powers threatened to do to defeated Turkey.

All these things had their repercussions in Afghanistan.

Of the unrest in India, and of the fulminations of

a British Prime Minister, there was born the Khilafat movement. The Faithful, absorbing the general atmosphere which was exceedingly critical of everything British, came to the conclusion that the Raj was an enemy of the Faith. Thousands of Moslems, therefore, determined to shake the dust of Hindustan from their shoes. There began the Hijrat—the departure from India of some 18,000 persons, all animated by the highest degree of religious zeal. Their route lay through Afghanistan.

This human flood suddenly welled up out of the inexhaustible millions of Hindustan, and flung itself against the barren hills of my country. The first series of waves were welcomed, and Amanullah received many plaudits because of the kindly nature of his reception. But this human flood threatened to overwhelm the country. All available land was apportioned to the immigrants, but still they continued to besiege the passes, and Amanullah was forced to refuse to allow more to enter.

As a result of this edict, many hundreds of religious zealots perished, and even in Afghanistan there were many who were not slow in declaring that the monarch had been guilty of inhospitality to the Faithful in the course which he pursued.

The Hijrat gave Amanullah a definite setback in the popular esteem of his countrymen, and provided the groundwork upon which much future criticism was based. Later, when he was to introduce his reforms, the Mullahs remembered his treatment of the Khilafatists, and made much capital out of the situation.

Then came the startling series of reforms—reforms which left the Afghans stupefied, and wondering what had come over this man who was now King.

Amanullah radically altered the means of collecting taxes, and schools were opened all over the country. Primary education was made compulsory, and in some of the schools the entire teaching was in German or French. Amanullah had in mind the time when the pupils of these schools would depart for the universities of France and Germany.

This educational scheme gave grave offence to the Mullahs who ordinarily had the education of the youthful in their own hands, and many of whom were deprived of their posts and mulcted of their emoluments.

Having given affront to a most powerful class, the King turned his attention to the hakims, or doctors. He gave orders that no one could practise medicine until he had passed the requisite examinations and been found efficient. This in itself was a revolutionary proceeding, and one which cut at the age-long customs of the people, and —one can do much with the Afghan, but it is advisable to leave precedent and custom alone.

Then, a new code of laws was prepared for the southern provinces. The code included the above reforms, but also another which caused the greatest misgivings and umbrage. Every eighth man was to be enlisted for compulsory military duty, and this cut across the class prejudices of very powerful families.

Out of this resentment grew the Khost rebellion in which I saw much active service as a soldier of Amanullah.

I wanted the excitement; I wanted to see modern troops in action, and generally I was out to learn, and to keep astride of events which I was sure were pointing in one direction, and one direction only.

The Mangal tribe was the first to rise. This was early in 1924. The Mangals were soon joined by others, and soon over six thousand revolutionaries had surrounded Matun, the capital of Khost. By the middle of April, most of the south was in open revolt.

There was one incident during the course of this revolt which gave me pause, and made me realise that the ways of kings and would-be kings can sometimes be hard.

In July, 1924, the grandson of Ameer Yakub Khan, one Abdul Karim, who had long been an exile in India, crossed the border to join the revolutionaries. He hoped that the name which he bore and the memory of his grandfather would cause the country to turn to him and to proclaim him as deliverer against one who sought to impose unpopular reforms. Abdul Karim was mistaken. No one evinced very much interest in him. He was politely received. His sword was accepted as an adjunct to the rebel forces, but he never became more than an individual.

There and then I decided that a name did not necessarily mean much, and that he who would be ruler of Afghanistan must be a person of resource and action.

After the Sulaiman Khails had joined the revolutionaries and had augmented the rebel forces by several thousand men, the skirmishing and long-range shooting which had been the order of the day developed into serious fighting.

I was in an engagement at Patka which was exceedingly sanguinary, neither side asking for quarter or expecting it. It was very hot going, especially when we were called upon to retire in the face of vastly superior numbers. I could not help but notice that the recalcitrant tribesmen fought with greater verve and enthusiasm than did the regular troops.

After our reverse at Patka engagements became general nearly every day, and I had my fill of campaigning, principally because there was no real zeal behind our attacks. For the main part we were outnumbered, but there was a reluctance among those in the higher commands to take ordinary military risks. It seemed to me that reputations were in greater count than mere military expediency.

As the rebel campaign progressed, the Government forces were pushed back to within a measurable distance of Kabul. It was then that the King decided to enlist the aid of tribesmen rival to those who had revolted—Khuganis, Afridis, Mohmunds, Kunaris, Shinwaris, Wazirs, Hazaras, and the like. These men, redoubtable fighters, received good pay and modern arms from Kabul, and their incursion into the fray unloosed so many tribal jealousies that recrimination and dissension overcame the rebel ranks. In this manner was the rebellion brought to a close. First one tribe submitted, and then another, not, I am afraid, to the force of arms, but in the face of feudal acrimony and the promises held out by Amanullah that the repugnant reforms would not be enforced.

During this campaign I was able to throw off many of the irksome restrictions of the barrack square, and to indulge in soldiering as I imagine soldiering is. My methods, which to the purely military class, appeared remarkably unorthodox, earned for me something of the reputation of a dare-devil, and certainly one for bravery. Yet, both were built entirely on my ability really to shoot and my refusal to be entrammelled by parade ground methods. I did not see anything particularly brave in stalking one who was addicted to inconvenient sniping, or in meeting shock tactics with shock tactics. If, during the course of an engagement it became embarrassingly obvious that I was being singled out for attack, then I, in my turn, singled out the attacker, and the best fighter won. My comrades called it bravery. I merely regarded it as common sense. Then, too, I had my amulet, and—there was still my destiny. Perhaps I could afford to take risks.

In January of the next year (1925) I was sent to Kabul with my unit, and on February 28, when the suppression of the revolt was circulated, I had my first view of Amanullah. Also, I saw Queen Suraya for the first time, for she appeared and made a speech to the returned soldiery. She presented me, with others, with a handkerchief in which were enfolded a number of silver coins.

There followed a reversion to barrack square ways which I found particularly trying after the freedom and licence of active service. Moreover, I considered that my reputation as a fighter and a shot should have been rewarded by more rapid promotion, and consequently higher pay. I found, however, an increasing disposition on the part of the paymaster to delay those parade days when money should be disbursed, and soon I, in company with the rest of the troops in Kabul, saw my pay considerably in arrears.

In these circumstances, I did not accept in too kindly a spirit the frequent chidings of my superiors, and bickerings and outspoken and definitely unmilitary language became general in my relations with others.

There was one officer, the equivalent to a major in rank, who took a particular delight in rendering my service unpalatable, and I, for my part, took particular care that my views on his military and other qualities should be freely aired.

If he could throw down scorn upon me when I was on parade, I could see that there were those who would snigger offensively when he passed through the streets, or was in the company of boon companions.

It was not difficult to engineer circumstances when a ribald and slanderous tongue could be overheard, to his shame and acute annoyance.

We did not love one another, and gradually this mutual ill-feeling grew into enduring hate. The man could never pass me on parade without giving off some slighting and derogatory remark—a state of affairs which was remarked upon by all and which did much to break down the discipline within my unit.

There had, of course, to come the day when this officer was particularly offensive and when he transcended all the bounds of decency and decorum.

Enraged beyond endurance by my actions in public, he made a bee line for me when on parade and gave himself over to the most objectionable commentary upon my personal and military bearing.

"These boors from the hills," he cried that all might hear. "See how they slouch. See, he carries his rifle as if it were a broom." This latter, of course, was a subtle way of conveying that in his opinion I was more accustomed to the ways of a broom than a rifle—a dire insult, as the direct insinuation was that I was of the sweeper caste.

He could see the blood boiling within me, and proceeded further to taunt me, and to such a degree that I could hear around me indignant murmurs which indicated, sufficiently clearly, that if anything untoward should occur, there would be no lack of sympathisers.

Suddenly, the bazaar-spawn advanced upon me, caught hold of my rifle, and shook it viciously into what he was pleased to term alignment.

I allowed it to slip back into the position it held before his interference, and again he grasped it. The man was panting with anger.

As he grasped the weapon for the second time, I released my hold, and brought up my hand to deliver a resounding smack on the side of his ugly face. Immediately, there was pandemonium. Some of the men broke ranks in their excitement, and crowded round, and the scene was more reminiscent of a bazaar fracas than a parade ground reproof.

Other officers and N.C.O.'s hurried to the spot, the major meanwhile gesticulating wildly and calling down the curses of heaven upon one who had so outraged his dignity in direct defiance to all precepts of the best military discipline.

Soon I found myself under arrest, and escorted to the guard room, charged with the crime of striking a superior officer on parade and with conduct prejudicial to good order and military discipline.

Seemingly, too, this officer was somewhat of a favourite, and the outlook was not as bright as it might have been.

I knew that my punishment would be the most severe which could be meted out to me, for no attempt was made to remove my manacles after I had been put safely behind the bars—a sure sign to the initiated that one is distinctly *non persona grata*.

However, I did not despair, for I still had my amulet, and Bacha Saquo had been in worse predicaments. Also, as I waited for darkness, I knew that those who had murmured in the ranks, headed by the faithful Jamal, would not be slow to evolve a plan which would ameliorate my lot.

It was two o'clock in the morning before I saw the cheerful features of Jamal. There had been some changing of the guard personnel, and his task had not been difficult. He had the irons from me in the space of a few seconds, and he was desperately anxious that I should immediately depart.

However, I had other views, for the guard room adjoined the armoury, and—I had to think of the pay that was due to me. In lieu of my rupees, I selected a rifle, and purloined four bandoliers containing over five hundred rounds of ·303 ammunition which, in the circumstances I considered a worthy exchange.

Just as I was departing from the armoury verandah, my eyes lighted on a canister. Gun cotton! I crept back. With Jamal tugging at my arm, I proceeded to the horse lines, and handing the bandoliers to my companion, advanced upon the sentry with complete effrontery.

The major sahib, I explained, required his charger. I, his orderly of the day, had orders to take it to him. Grumblingly, the man assisted me in saddling the beast, and also another required for the orderly who must accompany the major on his rounds of the posts.

I had to grin behind my hand. It was so childishly simple.

Thus armed and mounted, Jamal would have us away to the hills, but still I tarried.

"The moon is not bright," I said, "and this is the hour when all men sleep heavily. Why this haste?"

Refusing to be skurried out of Kabul, I made my way, followed by a protesting Jamal, to this major's house. It was an imposing structure and befitted one who robbed the troops of their pay and their rations, and I already knew something of its layout.

The night was hot, and there was the major lying in the open in his compound upon a gaily-coloured string charpoi. Gazing over the wall, I chuckled, for the man was attired in a single sheet-like garment, for greater comfort and for coolness. Dropping to the ground, I scouted round until I found a chicken's feather, then scaled the wall.

Approaching the sleeper with my hillman's stealth, I crouched beside his cot, and gently I tickled his side.

With a sleepy movement of protest, he rolled over on his side, and he was half uncovered. Giving him a few moments' respite in order that he might sink again deeply into slumber, I applied the feather gently to the other side, and again he rolled. Carefully, and with infinite caution, I snatched his covering, and was over the wall.

From my canister I took two wads of guncotton. One I placed against the wall near the major, and another by the wall surrounding his women's quarters. Lighting some hastily manufactured fuses, I retired a short distance to watch.

The resultant explosion was satisfying and commendable. The noise in itself was sufficient to set all Kabul by the ears, to turn out all the guards, to wake up all the pariah dogs, and to cause hundreds to come tumbling from their repose to investigate the cause of this unwonted disturbance.

While alarm bugles brayed, dogs barked, men cursed and women screamed, I waited for the dust to settle to reveal the outcome of my handiwork. From my place of concealment it was difficult to restrain my guffaws. The walls surrounding the officer's sleeping compound had been almost entirely demolished, and that by his women's quarters sufficient to reveal the women of his household running frenziedly for safety, absolutely unveiled and quite impervious to the rude gaze of the populace.

As for the major, he sat on the side of his bed in a kind of mental haze, gazing with horror-struck eyes at the scene of desolation around him, and then at his bare limbs and undraped torso.

He was so obviously torn by a desire to rush out upon and destroy those who had invaded his privacy, and to hide the shortcomings of his non-existent attire that I could have screamed with suppressed joy.

He continued to sit there, wriggling painfully, doing his feeble utmost to hide his nakedness, while the crowds surged round, gazing their fill.

It was most satisfactory.

I had blackened more than the major's face.

And, the comments he had to endure!

The crowd was angry that a man should so forget himself as to parade his body in such circumstances.

"Who is this low-born ruffian," they asked loudly and insistently, "who so forgets his Faith that he appears in public unclothed?"

"Who is this whose women show themselves unveiled?"

It was good. Very good.

CHAPTER VI

I RETURN TO KOHISTAN

At the time of which I speak, the Bolsheviks were filling their propaganda schools at Tashkent, and elsewhere, with material from Hind and Afghanistan, but judging by the efforts of Jamal, methinks they were wasting their time.

With considerable misgivings I had decided to return at long last to my native Kohistan. In this I was prompted both by Jamal, and the force of circumstances. When I reminded Jamal of the manner in which I had left my village, he said little, beyond suggesting that the passage of time had perhaps healed a number of wounds. I, however, could not be so sanguine, for there was that attack on the woman to be considered. That of the Bunya Hindu, and the theft of his jewellery, came into a far different and lesser category.

We wasted little time in shaking off the dust of the capital from our shoes, and I must admit that the major had a pretty taste in horseflesh. The animal upon which I was mounted was superb in its action, and a delight to ride when it came to the mountain paths of my home province where a horse was required to possess the fleetness of the gazelle, the sure-footedness of the mule, and the climbing abilities of the goat. The major's charger (now mine) possessed all these attributes, and more. I

often wondered what he paid for him, or whether
he, too, obtained possession by devious ways.

That ridden by Jamal was swift, but in other
respects but passable. Mine was a steed on which
to covort unheedingly down mountain crags, and
across boulder-strewn river beds. With uncanny
precision this magnificent beast would implant a
dainty hoof on the one square inch of earth which
would support our combined weight with safety,
and would ignore, with a presagement which never
ceased to intrigue me, those snares and pitfalls
which are the lot of less finely balanced creatures.

We had come to the hill ranges which gave on
to my village, and my mind was occupied by many
a dubious thought. Should I boldly descend upon
the village, and announce my homecoming, or
should I send Jamal forward as an ambassador to
spy out the land.

As we lay up in the hills, I espied a small body of
horsemen approaching from afar, and presently I
recognised the Elder, now incredibly withered, but
still virile and haughty, to whom I had presented
the over-ripe peach.

I decided that here was the means to test the
reactions to my presence in the neighbourhood. I
expected nothing but abuse and revilings from this
old curmudgeon, but by the mere intensity or otherwise of his vituperations would I be able to judge
of much that I wanted to know.

With a word to Jamal, we hobbled our horses,
and bound their muzzles, and placed ourselves in
a position where we could intercept this party bound
for our village.

I allowed it to get within forty yards of us before revealing myself, and with the head which I silently protruded there was the muzzle of my wicked looking rifle.

"Tobah!" exclaimed old peach face testily, when he saw that rifle so nonchalantly aimed in his direction. "Who would have the ill-grace to hold up the Faithful within sight of their home village. Who would place this indignity upon the grey hairs of an old man?"

I watched him peering under his turban, saying not a word; then I saw him start, and a brighter look came into his eyes.

"Do I not know that face?" he exclaimed, turning to those with him—those who were cast to stone by the cold grimace of that rifle muzzle.

They forebore to answer, but the old man was not to be gainsaid. Even with the rifle pointed at him he took a step forward, the better to see, then his aged face became wreathed in an astonishing array of smiles.

"It is that vagrant, Bacha," he cried, jubilation in his voice.

"He has returned amongst us, and must needs play his pranks upon the Elders."

Peach face was quite urbane, but I was suspicious.

"O, Bacha," he cried again. "Welcome home, you profligate, and tell us how you have waxed rich with the Ferenghi.

"Welcome home," he continued, "the young man who so steadfastly upheld our tribal honour!"

I was amazed by this display, but, carrying my rifle, I advanced to greet the ancient Elder.

He patted me on the back, and gave little chirrups of joy. The old boy was manifestly pleased to see me. Out of the corner of my eye I could see Jamal grinning.

The old one went on:

"Thy companion, Jamal Gul, wrote and told us of thy plight with that pestiferous Nur Khan. We know how you so bravely followed him when he robbed the Hindu moneylender and killed that man and very nearly his wife. The chowkidar, too, added his testimony, my son, for he too saw you going.

"It was a valiant deed, O Bacha, for one so young to encompass this bad one's death. Honour is yours. There shall be feasting when we reach the village!"

Such was the manner of my homecoming.

My father, the water carrier, was well nigh dead of old age, and another sprinkled water in his stead, but that did not prevent the feasting which the old one had promised.

Round the village fires that night, the villagers gorged on mountain sheep, goats and a wild variety of pillaus, and I was fêted as the upholder of honour, and the slayer of he who had killed the money lender.

When the first enthusiasm had worn a little thin, there were those who patiently expected more to the entertainment, and did little to hide their impatience.

"Come, O Bacha," they cried. "Display thee of thy wealth. Show us that which you have filched from the Ferenghi—thou who hast dwelt in the rich land of Hindustan."

I who had a horse, a rifle and five hundred rounds of ammunition and hardly a cowrie besides, felt uncomfortable. I attempted to laugh and to joke, but these people expected a returned traveller from Hind to be rich, and said so.

There were long faces, and not a few derisive comments when I woefully explained that I had lost of my riches in gaming in the bazaars of Jalalabad, and that since my decision to fight for Amanullah, there had been few opportunities of amassing wealth.

The village wits waxed hilarious at my expense, and even went so far as to suggest that I had allowed a sleepy Ferenghi to get the better of a hillman, and that Bacha Saquo, the smart one, was not so clever after all.

But, when appraising my possessions, I had forgotten something. That which encircled my arm had slipped my memory. Suddenly the words of the Mullah came back to me, and inflamed by the taunts of the villagers, I stood upright in the glare of the fires in order that all might see, and held up my hand, commanding silence.

"You scoff at a warrior," I said harshly. "You scoff at one who has stolen rifles and horses from the Ferenghi—something which all will agree is worthy, and no easy task. You scoff at one who has fought in the late war with the men of Khost, and —you scoff because you are numbskills. You scoff at a warrior who is learning his trade, and—who has ever known of an apprentice who was rich?"

I made a gesture, and tossed a meagre handful of rupees into the flames.

"There," I said fiercely, "you have my regard for a few pieces of silver. Silver means nothing to Bacho Saquo. The treasures which I amassed in Hind meant nothing to me, else—why should I have sported them away?

"You see before you," I added grandiloquently, "one who is to be the ruler of this land—one who is to occupy the throne at Kabul, and one who will be your master. Take heed then, before you scoff, for Bacha Saquo has a long memory, and in the fulness of time you may regret your hilarity."

A great shout of laughter greeted my words, in which the Peach face joined with gusto.

"Bacha is a droll," he exclaimed through his convulsions. "He has learned to be amusing in the land of the Ferenghi.

Again I held up my hand, for I was angered.

"You laugh," I cried furiously, "but the day of which I speak will come. It has been ordained."

With what dignity I could muster, I sat down, ignoring the vapid twitterings of the delighted villagers, and rejecting with scorn further offers from the well-filled fleshpots.

Actually, I was mad with mortification that I should have been goaded into revealing my secret, for there was no denying the fact. These good people were firmly of the opinion that I was mad. I resolved that mad or not, they should have cause to remember Bacha Saquo.

There was, of course, no life for me in the village. There was no escape for one who had seen something of the world, and who saw on every hand the narrowness of outlook which was the lot of those I had previously regarded with awe, and even respect. Now I found their oft-spoken views childish and irksome, and I longed to be away upon the hillsides with my good horse under me, and with my rifle and five hundred rounds.

Also, wherever I went in the village streets, I was met with a mock deference, and ironic greetings of "Badshah," and this became too much for my proud spirit.

Soon, we were away.

And now did Fortune once more turn her face toward me, for I went abroad from where the hills were high, to those beyond, which were lower and where, lying secreted in the rough boulder country, I could watch the dust of slowly moving caravans.

Yes, the caravans. But here, they were well armed, and the merchants were well protected. What could one person do with but one rifle. True, there was Jamal, but there must be more.

Of the men of my village there were none I would take into my confidence. There I was too well known. There, men still saw the Bacha of old when they beheld me, and the Bacha who made a fool of himself on the night of the feast.

No, I must have men upon whom I could impress my personality, and the villagers were not for me.

Still, to depart into the beyond, to recruit for enterprises such as I had in mind was difficult. It was one asking for death should I fail, and one calling for cunning and for guile at the best. Once I had made a footing, the rest I knew would be easy. There are always those who will join the train of a successful freebooter; aye—and always those ready to shoot him down in order to secure the leadership, and the greater share of the loot which goes with this position of pre-eminence.

To go forth upon the hillsides and calmly ask for recruits was impossible. There would be those who already ravaged the caravan routes, ready at once to blot out the upstart, who thought to impinge upon their preserves; for the newcomer to the honourable trade of freebooting must needs fight not only the soldiery which accompany the merchants, but also those who are apt to display jealousy and resentment.

Many a would-be caravan robber has passed to the beyond before ever firing a shot, or getting within striking distance of his rich quarry.

Jamal, to whom I confided my thoughts, had few suggestions to offer, and none which would hold water.

I resolved, therefore, to rely entirely upon my destiny, and the protection accorded by my amulet and the goodly rifle which I treasured and caressed like a trusty friend.

"Come, Jamal," I said, when I was unable further to contain myself in the village, "prepare for further travels. Go and beg, steal or borrow food, and prepare our horses, for to-morrow, at dawn, we try a throw with Fate."

"But," Jamal expostulated, "you have a rifle—you have ammunition. I—I have not so much as a dagger."

"Who," I returned, "has the best rifle in the village?"

"Ahmad Khan," he replied without hesitation.

"And, ammunition?"

He nodded.

I patted him on the arm.

"Be ready, Jamal," I said confidently. "You shall be armed. Ahmad Khan shall supply the deficiency. Bacha Saquo has spoken."

That night, armed with a knife and a blanket, I went to the house of Ahmad Khan. The walls of his house were of mud, and carefully I scraped a hole near the door. With my body over the hole, I was careful to exclude all draughts from the outer air, and then inserted my hand. To unfasten the door was simple. Placing the blanket over the hole, still to exclude the wind, I crept inside. I could hear Ahmad Khan sleeping peacefully.

With great caution, I struck a match, and for about a second and a half allowed its illumination to fill the room. Ahmad Khan stirred, but did not wake, and I saw his rifle by his bedside.

Between me and my objective were two goats, one asleep, and the other contentedly chewing. There were various brass vessels also there to trap the unwary, and then the light went out. Every detail of that room was clear in my mind. But the goat which was chewing! Would it remain content, or would it rise with awkwardness of goats and give a bleating and all revealing "Blah"?

It did neither. I believe it went to sleep.

I took the rifle, and also the bandolier of ammunition which was beside it.

I made Ahmad Khan a present of the blanket. I would not have him catch a chill from the night air, for he was but lightly covered.

Then, there were the goats. I was certain that he would have felt amiss had the aroma been allowed to dissipate.

Who says there is not good in Bacha Saquo?

CHAPTER VII

OVER THE HILLS

THE way of the caravan robber is to waylay the merchants as they pass through some rocky defile. Suddenly, from the hillsides, a burst of fire will be sent over the heads of the trailing company, and all is immediate confusion. Should any of the armed escort show fight, they are immediately shot down. More often than not, however, the escort disappears amidst the welter of surprised and struggling animals, and only emerges, valiantly to throw challenges at a departing enemy, when the richest merchants have been despoiled and the caravan is deficient of its most richly comparisoned camels and horses.

Caravan robbers invariably act thus, for the hillsides lend of the element of surprise, and in such terrain it is easy to post forward parties who will rush forward, secure the animals to prevent a stampede, and overawe the protesting merchants and the cringing or otherwise guards before there has been time for scattered wits to collect themselves.

Such is the easy way, and for such enterprises a band of stalwarts of at least twenty is required. All have to be nicely drilled. Each man has to know his part, and there has to be perfect co-ordination.

I, Bacha Saquo, had to seek another way, and now it was Jamal who said I was mad.

I would ride forward beyond the hills, and take what I wanted on the plains.

I reasoned thus: I had no men—as yet, and I had to evolve unorthodox means.

By long and bitter experience, the merchants knew what was likely to be their fate in the passes, and were prepared. No lone wolf would stand a chance there, and the armed guards would seize upon the opportunity with avidity to vindicate their valour. They would dispose of this "Army" of robbers, and demand extra pay for their martial triumph.

No, the only chance for Bacha was to engineer some scheme which would catch the prey before it arrived in the field of suspense and suspicion; when, indeed, the guards would be no guards, but only hangers-on, and the merchants too full of their money plans and good food even to entertain the idea of danger.

That was the main theme. But the details?

These required more than care. Inspiration was called for, for I was about to attempt something which, over the centuries, the caravan robbers had laid by as impossible and unfruitful.

We had two men, two horses and now, thanks to Ahmad Khan, two rifles. Not a large force, in all conscience, and not an overpowering armament. But, these merchants had to deal with Bacha, who was the best shot in the Afghan army, and with a horse whose paces were supreme.

Also, Bacha had made a study of war. Even when obeying the vituperative drill officer was he thinking. And, he had seen much of the British paltans in their war exercises in the vicinity of Peshawar. Bacha was not one to go through life with his eyes shut.

This, I admit, was all vainglory. Of all this I spoke to impress Jamal, for still I had no scheme. Yet, I was sure, one would come.

It did.

Yet, Jamal thought I was mad.

For my purpose I had to select a small caravan. A large one would have defeated my purpose, and would have rendered my task impossible. What I wanted was a convoy of less than one hundred and fifty camels, and I set out to find it.

I was out to achieve fame, to be known throughout the Kohistan country as a fighter and a bravo, but for weeks my opportunity eluded me.

We rode forth beyond the hills, and watched the caravans with their rich spoil, for we had to be our own spies, and to provide our own intelligence. At last there came that which I required—a caravan of convenient size, not too heavily armed, yet giving fair promise of loot and gain.

All that day, hovering in the distance upon its flank, we trailed it, Jamal gazing upon me askance, and wondering when I would give the work to attack. But such was not my way.

Next morning we rode ahead, and I selected terrain which was devoid of character and which lacked anything of a formidable character behind which could lurk a possible enemy.

Here, I reasoned, where danger could not possibly be, the merchants would lay aside their cares, and the guards, more likely than not, would be riding

with all thought of attack far from their minds.
Their arms would be in the saddle bags, or at least,
far from the ready.

Jamal and I rode on, and I selected two places
each side of the caravan trail where, ordinarily,
even a jackal could not hide. With our hands, and
aided by my knife, we proceeded to dig—not a
difficult operation in the flat, sandy terrain. I had
seen the British soldiery act similarly, and—I had
a plan.

We developed holes, each large enough to contain
a human body when lying prone, and over the
holes I distributed saddle cloths from our saddlery,
and pinned them down with stones. Over the
cloths I sprinkled earth and sand, and anyone
coming even within the distance of a yard, would
have passed by unknowing. From the caravan
trail these hide-outs were quite impossible to detect.
I was pleased with my handiwork.

When the dust of the caravan was seen in the
distance, we hied to our holes, and waited.

To Jamal I had given his instructions. He was to
fire like many men, but he was to take care not to
hit or maim, unless the situation got beyond my
control, and hitting became necessary. Following
my first shots, he was to put up a barrage of
musketry, and to send his bullets whistling over
the ears of the merchants and their guards. Other
than that, he must use his discretion, and be guided
by me.

The hide-outs which I had selected were about
two hundred yards each side of the trail. They were
near enough for quick and accurate shooting, but

not near enough to be overwhelmed by any sudden rush. Our horses we hid behind a small hillock about a mile from the road.

We lay there silently, and I watched the caravan approach. As I surmised, there was nothing in the attitude of the men to indicate suspicion or alarm. The merchants jogged along on their fat ponies, laughing, grumbling, and talking; others were perched on their camels, and the guards, for the main part, were walking, with their arms slung across various beasts of burden.

Now was the crucial time approaching, with the head of the caravan almost level, and all depended upon the first few tense seconds. Indeed, the whole matter would be one of seconds. If it were not, it would spell dire, abject failure.

My object, of course, was not to capture the entire caravan. Such is beyond the scope of even the largest and best organised bands of robbers. I wanted sufficient to provide me with temporary opulence. More than that, I wanted proof of the fact that Bacha Saquo was not a mere braggart.

I passed the entire line under inspection, and I was pleased. Leading, were thirty or more camels, each treading in each other's footsteps, the one behind being tethered to the tail of the one ahead.

Following this initial party, was another of five camels, similarly tethered, and I was pleased to note that these were good animals and loaded in a manner which indicated that the merchant whose goods they carried was a man of substance. Behind came further camels in groups, all tied, and a mixed medley of horses, pack mules, and donkeys.

I decided that the five well-laden camels would be sufficient for my purpose.

These unsuspecting caravan men were to receive a shock. Entirely out of the blue, there came a shot. The leader of the five camels which I had chosen as mine own, crashed to the ground with a bullet in its brain. The other four, kicked and plunged like ships in a storm, but their tethering ropes held. Quick as light, I fired again, and this time at the second camel in the leading string. I had noted with some satisfaction that it was not one of those which bore a string muzzle. I sighted carefully, for much depended upon this shot, and the bullet went home, through the animal's tail just where it meets the body.

With a plunge and a scream of rage and agony, the animal swerved, and the rope tethering it to the third in the string became taut, tweaking its maltreated member so that the camel screamed again. It went mad; it went berserk. It thrust forward, insane with rage and hurt, and buried its fearsome teeth into the haunches of the leader.

I commenced then a real fusillade, sending the bullets whining by the ears of the bewildered caravan men. Jamal chimed in with gusto, and the noise and the confusion lent the atmosphere of a sanguinary battle.

In the caravan line, all was terror and confusion. The leading string was absolute pandemonium.

A guard, more perplexed or braver than the rest, rushed for his rifle, and actually had it in his hands before I detected him. I aimed a careful shot at the metal on the weapon's stock. I wanted blood,

noise and terror rather than death. The result was
satisfactory. The rifle was snatched from his hands
as if by some invisible fiend, and parts of the stock
spattered the man's face. I could see him wiping
the blood from his eyes wondering from where
came this strange visitation.

Then, what I had counted upon happened. The
shouting and the screaming and the firing was too
much for the leading camels. He who had been
punctured through the tail was still burying his
teeth in the flanks of the leader, and that worthy
decided that he had had enough. With a snort and
a scream, he started off at his lolloping canter, and
the rest began to follow. Soon the dust rose high,
and from a canter it became a gallop and a veritable
stampede. Bullets flung after the hindermost helped
to lend energy to action where it promised to be
lethargic, and the sight was good.

Men rode and ran alongside the frightened animals,
shouting and beating in a vain effort to stop the
rout. Their endeavours only urged on the terror-
stricken beasts to more determined action.

Soon, there was nothing left but a cloud of fast
settling dust, five lone camels, one of which
was dead, and a man, obviously the owner of
the merchandise who stood by them, wringing
his hands, and crying lustily for succour and
support.

A bullet nipped at the dust between his feet, and
he jumped. Another bit the dust within an inch of
his toe, and he backed. Another crashed into the
ground just on the spot where he was about to step
and flinging up his arms, and crying shrilly, he ran

up the caravan trail after those who had so expeditiously departed.

Jamal and I emerged to inspect our gains. Four camels, tied in an almost inextricable knot, were arrested to the spot by the weight of the one who was dead. And, all were well laden. There were choice carpets, rich spices, wondrous silks, rough silver ingots and expensive unguents. It was a good haul.

Working with speed, Jamal and I loaded the dead camel's pack on to the backs of the protesting four, and struck out at a tangent to the road for the security of the hills.

Three days later we arrived at our village by circuitous routes. Our way was long, and specially determined, not because we expected pursuit or reprisals, but because there were many who would have been pleased to have relieved us of the results of my guile.

Our arrival was the signal for much jubilation, and for no few expressions of wonder.

When Jamal told the tale of our exploits around the evening fires, there were some who are first refused to believe, but—there were the camels, and there was the loot. What better proof could there be?

There was a new difference displayed toward Bacha Saquo when he walked abroad, for he who could fight a caravan practically single-handed was a man of note.

In the disposal of my wares, I decided to deal through one whom I knew in Peshawar, and when the time came to despatch them I bade Jamal write a letter. Only he and I knew the contents, and only he and I knew how much of the proceeds of my first freebooting gesture I was expending on the future.

Presently, sundry small and mysterious bundles arrived for me from the land of Hind, and again I was prepared to take the road.

This time Jamal and I were not to be alone, for seven men had approached me in the watches of the night and begged to be allowed to join Bacha in his raids upon the wealthy. Six of these I selected. The seventh, whom I did not trust over much, I told to present himself at some later time when I might find use for his services. Disgruntled, the man went his way, but he performed, quite unwittingly, the part which I had assigned him. The word went round that Bacha Saquo was particular and preferential, and that the ragtail and bobtail need not apply to him for employment.

Again, and not a little to the consternation of those who had thrown in their lot with me, I determined to thrust at fate on the plains rather than in the confines of the hills, but this time I wanted more than the packs of five camels. I was after an entire caravan—something which had never been attempted by any of the hills robbers through the ages. By a really bold stroke I was determined to establish myself.

Again we journeyed forth beyond the hills, and beyond even the scene of my first essay on the caravan route. Ten miles distant from there was a caravanserai where the caravans were wont to remain for rest and refreshment for the night. It was on this caravanserai that I concentrated my plans.

I found, by watching from the distance, that the caravans arrived at a late hour, usually just as dusk was merging into the night, for the trek from the previous halting place was a long one. This I regarded as a fortuitous circumstance, and one which must be bent to my will.

From my place of concealment, I watched more than one caravan file in before I completed my plans, then I acted.

In the distance I could discern slowly approaching a train of some two hundred camels. These, with their heavy burdens, I resolved should be mine.

I judged, glancing at the fast disappearing sun, that this caravan would be later than usual in reaching its objective, and I made my dispositions accordingly.

With the approach of dusk my men and I closed in on the caravanserai, and when the caravan filed in to its night's resting place I had men on both sides, and at a distance of not more than fifty yards.

Distinctly, we could hear the grunts and thuds of the camels, as they sank to the ground beneath their burdens, and the cursing and revilings of tired men who had to deal with animals who were churlish and obstreperous.

Then I gave the signal—my old one of the jackal, thrice repeated, and the caravanserai suddenly became illuminated in dazzling, garish light.

Verey light pistols, appropriated from the British in Peshawar and along the posts of the Khyber,

gushed forth their weird streams of coloured radiance.
The like had never been seen by these men before,
and momentarily they were struck dead with
amazement.

Then the voice of Jamal rose loudly among them.
"It is the sign," he shrieked, "the sign. The
heavens are pouring their vengeance upon us.
Woe! Woe! Fly, fly my brothers. The heavens
enact vengeance."

Streams of red, white and green light continued
to shower over the affrighted men, and loud rose
their voices in fear and alarm.

Exhorted by the leathern-lunged Jamal, there
were those who stampeded. They rushed blindly
forth to escape from this accursed spot, and their
fear communicated itself to the others. In a few
moments the entire company was fleeing down the
road from whence it came, and one of my men
followed them up to give them a further taste of
these wild lights of the Powers of Darkness.

The camels, disturbed by the commotion, had
for the main part rumbled and grumbled to their
feet, and when we closed in upon them, there was
Jamal already slashing with his knife. He was
following the line of still tethered animals, and
was removing the bells from the necks of the leaders.
There was not much we had forgotten.

Led by Jamal, the first camels began protestingly
to emerge from the caravanserai, and four other
men assisted him in urging on the long line.

When all had silently departed, and had been
swallowed up in the darkness, I fell back upon the
roadway where the firing of Verey lights led me

to my man. When I reached him, his stock of ammunition was near exhausted. Him I despatched for our horses.

Lying there in the darkness, I could hear an occasional grunt and gurgle in the distance as the camels were led away from the road at right angles to the trail, and I could hear also the confused murmur of voices in the distance.

Winded by their headlong flight, the fat merchants, out of reach of those awe-inspiring lights, had halted to take stock of the situation. I realised that it could not be long before the more resolute among them would be haranguing the guards, and demanding an immediate return to the camp. So it must be in the ordinary nature of things, and so it transpired.

There were wild and angry shouts in the distance as the argument persisted, and I smiled as I visualised the broadsides with which the goodly merchants would be raking their paid hirelings, the guards. I could visualise also, the protestations of valour and bravery which these men would be making.

The tumult and the shouting suddenly gave over to a lower and more sustained note, and I knew that a decision had been reached, and it had been resolved to return to the caravanserai and brave the phenomenon should it reoccur. I could hear the voices coming nearer, and presently I could make out, some eighty yards away, a dense mass of men, all hugging close together for their better protection.

Sixty—fifty—forty yards I allowed them to come, and then I acted.

I had in mind a British bomb for which I had had to pay the extravagant price of three hundred and fifty rupees. But, if all went well, I would deem the money well spent.

The instructions which I had received with this strange instrument of death bade me pull forth the pin, and count four. I extracted the contrivance, and counted—somewhat rapidly, I confess, then hurled it into the midst of the advancing horde.

For an interminable period I judged that my money had been misplaced and that the much vaunted Ferenghi were less clever in the arts of war than we imagined. With a blood-curdling "Whoof," however, the bomb did its work, and the air was filled with noise. There were groans, and shrieks, and cries of unfettered alarm, and the whole band was in confusion, not knowing from whence had come this terrible visitation,· and not knowing which way to flee.

But, even yet I had not finished. I, Bacha, had still to see the result of my handiwork. From my clothes I snatched forth a powerful torch, and directed it upon the shrieking throng. I pressed my thumb, and there was an intense illumination. A dozen men were upon the ground. Some were still, and others were threshing round in a welter of blood.

For the rest, the torch meant the end. There was sent up into the evening sky one long cry of apprehension and terror, and those who could run, or walk, or crawl, made the best speed possible along the road which they had come.

It was enough. I knew that I had won. Those

men, notwithstanding their fatigue, would not stop until they fell in their tracks, or until they reached the camping ground they had left that morning.

I, Bacha Saquo, was free from pursuit.

In the morn, the wild land of Kohistan would ring with the tales of his dare-devilry and success. He would not lack for retainers, and he would be a power in the land.

CHAPTER VIII

MASTER

MEN flocked to the train of Bacha Saquo, and his name was known throughout the hills of Kohistan, but Bacha, still with his amulet, allowed his aspirations to soar.

Yes, I saw myself as the most successful robber of the countryside, and men on all hands bowed and did me honour, but—that was because I could distribute largesse, and could guarantee to those who accompanied me on my forays a handsome return for their endeavours.

Bacha Saquo wanted more than this. He desired the mastery, and would have it.

It is not to be supposed that my incursion into the ranks of the successful was viewed with any enthusiasm by those who regarded the looting of the caravans as a long-vested interest, and there was one in particular who displayed his umbrage.

He was Sharfuddin, who had for long regarded himself as King of the Passes, and he watched with a wry face my snatching of the loot from beneath his nose. Moreover, he made it a personal matter. He declared that Bacha Saquo was blackening his face, and was making a fool of him before the people of Kohistan.

It was not for me to argue upon or dispute this point, but the fact remained that as long as this man remained, he denied me the position of pre-eminence which I desired. With Sharfuddin out of the way I should be undisputed master, and there would be none who could question my actions. As it was, I had to move with a certain circumspection which was irritating. Always had I to be certain that Sharfuddin was not on my flank, for, given the opportunity, he would destroy me.

But, how to dispose of this thorn of the flesh? The man was too subtle, too full of guile to give me open combat upon the hills. His way was the ambush, and—his following was equal in numbers to mine. No, there must be some other way.

I resolved that I would attack and plunder this man's village. Dashing tactics, and the unexpected, had served me well in the past. I would again adopt the course farthest from the minds of men, for in the hills, although village may set upon village in the fire of feudal ire, robbers leave the villagers severely alone, mainly because the villagers would consolidate after the raid, and fall upon the robber bands from an ambush and destroy them.

But I decided when I had finished with Sharfuddin there should be no village. The hand of Bacha Saquo would fall, and the result would be there for the whole land to see. Thereafter, I would be master.

My band now consisted of over one hundred men, for the word had gone out that here was a new leader, allegiance to whom promised a rich harvest; and day by day other men came.

To Jamal I proposed my plan of ensnaring Sharfuddin in his own lair, and he was definitely against the venture. To others, too, of my band I whispered of my plans, and they also were pessimistic. Yet I spoke of the time when I had raided a caravan practically single-handed, and of the time when I had captured one entire with but a handful of men. I boasted, and assured all of success, yet being Bacha, I did not rush straight forth into the hills, waving my sword and firing my rifle. There were other ways.

True, I went forth upon the hills, but I went alone, and in the guise of a traveller from Hind making his unpretentious way across the passes. None would have recognised Bacha in the poor, travel-stained garments which I affected.

The people of Sharfuddin's village made me welcome, for they were far from the caravan routes, and news of the outside world filtered through to them but slowly. Three days and three nights I tarried among them, telling of what I had seen, and giving these people news. In some cases it was months old, yet they had not heard, and welcomed all that I had to say.

As I slowly perambulated the village, I made good use of my eyes. I marked down the abodes of those who were Sharfuddin's principal lieutenants, for these houses gave promise of rich rewards. In the main, however, my seemingly casual eye took in the defences which, even for a village of its character, were secure and stout, and capable of maintaining a stiff resistance to the batterings of an invader.

Indeed, it was no light task that I had set myself.

The walls of the village were thick, and strong, and in good repair, and the watch towers were massive, and were well manned each night. At nightfall, the gates were closed, and none might enter the village, and the watchmen were so vigilant that none could approach within one hundred yards of the walls without being challenged, and perchance fired upon.

Indeed, it was no light task.

I departed from the village at the expiration of three days with a clear picture of its defences upon my mind, but, as yet, no constructive plan.

Two nights later, when tossing miserably upon my bed, the idea came to me, and I cursed myself for the tardiness of my brain for, indeed, it was so simple.

My principal weapon of attack must be diversion, and the more noise that was encompassed, the better for my purpose. But, the matter of that diversion—that which would draw the night watch from its ceaseless vigil upon the ramparts!

Soon the village of Sharfuddin had another visitor—yet another traveller—and when he departed, for he did not tarry over long, he went when the evening shades were casting their shadows. Also, he went accompanied by a village dog, which he had enticed beyond the walls with specially prepared bits of liver such as no dog can withstand. The disappearance of the dog would, of course, be marked, but none would give over much attention to such a detail. Even the owner would merely shrug his shoulders, and murmur: "That shaitan— he roams again."

In my own village all was feverish preparation. We made rope ladders with hooks, we made pads for our horses' hoofs, and to each bridle there was looped a length of turban which would eventually bind the muzzle which might give out an all-revealing neigh.

Then, on the night when there was no moon, we set out, timing our riding so that we should appear in the vicinity of the village about half-way through the vigil of the second watch; when men sleep their deepest, and watchmen yawn.

Tethered to a stake upon the hillside was the village dog. We collected him, but he did not march with us. It was a lone man who saw to his wants, and led him by the rope back in the direction of his village.

Half a mile short of our objective, we dismounted, and our advance thereon was conducted with extreme caution. We went forward like snakes, and as silently, and halted within two hundred yards of the walls. We awaited the signal.

In our train we had one of our own village dogs, and he had a part to perform. Just beyond the orbit of vision of the guardsmen, and on the side of the village farthest from that which we would attack, he was introduced to the other. Carefully were they tethered, and firmly, and each had a sufficiency of movement. But, when they strained, their muzzles were distant an inch of each other, and the ropes held.

No self-respecting village dog will brook intrusion by another, and no dog allowed the run of my village will fail to take up a challenge, and the result was excellent.

These dogs howled, growled and yapped, and worked themselves into a fury because they were denied the privilege of burying their fangs in each other. Moreover, because of my stratagem, the uproar was constant, and its venue did not vary. This was no running fight, and this fact and its very intensity drew all the watchmen to the farthest wall that they might peer into the darkness and discuss the strange visitation.

With this novel signal, we advanced, knives at the ready, and we entered the village without opposition.

Competent hands stretched forth to deal from the rear with the unsuspecting watchmen, and others crept from house to house in the village disposing of all males who came without the category of boy.

We were well through with our pleasurable task before stealth need be abandoned, and a remnant of the village took up the fight. It was short and sharp, this encounter, and in the exchange of shots, we lost several men, yet the issue was never in doubt, for word soon went round that Sharfuddin was dead.

Indeed, the remaining villagers could not doubt the fact, for I, Bacha Saquo, had disposed of him, and I led the attack with his head perched upon a pole. It made a devastating battering ram, and its presence did much to take the fight out of those who would offer continued resistance.

With the sacking and the demolition of Sharfuddin's village and the summary slaying of the leader himself and of all his men, I became the undisputed ruler of the mountains. All men did me honour, not because of what they might receive in riches, but because they deemed it wise. And that is real power.

When the name of Bacha Saquo was mentioned in the villages, the people trembled. My star was rising.

It is not to be supposed that Kabul went in ignorance of my activities. On the contrary, there was every reason to suppose that the capital was well informed, more especially as a month after the incident of Sharfuddin's dismissal, my spies reported that a military force was on its way to seek me out and to exact vengeance for the insult placed upon the Crown.

By this time I commanded the allegiance of every able-bodied man within a radius of thirty miles, and the news left me cold. Indeed, except to enquire the position of this force, and its strength, I did nothing to combat its advance until it was within my sphere of influence.

Why should I have done otherwise? I was secure; I could bide my time; I had an adequate force, and why should I do battle away from my own door-step? Whenever possible, I like to do these things in comfort. Besides, quite unknowingly, this Government punitive force was bringing me a present. I did not want the trouble of unnecessary transport.

The Government force turned out to be a company of two hundred men under two officers. Besides regulation rifles, it had an armament of two machine-guns—and I coveted those machine-guns.

In the fulness of time their capture was ridiculously easy, for these arrogant Kabulis rather disdained their task of routing out a tribal robber. They regarded the affair in the light of sport, but—they had left Kabul before the arrival there of vital information, and they were quite unaware of my strength. They were under the impression that all they had to do was to precipitate themselves upon my village, overawe it with their machine-guns, and demand my surrender.

They were mistaken.

Eleven miles from my village there is a suitable defile for the disposal of arrogant Government forces, and there I repaired with but a handful of my men. To take a large force would be to show the tribesmen around me that I took this Government intervention seriously. Actually, I scoffed at anything the Government might attempt.

In this defile, I copied the tactics which had proved so successful when I made my first descent upon the caravan routes.

Disdaining the officer, I put bullets, in quick succession, through the heads of the two mules transporting the machine-guns. With these mules were twenty-one others, grouped together in threes.

Seven shots rang out with the rapidity of light, and there was not a miss. Seven mules fell, and as they fell they chained to the spot the fourteen others. On the backs of those mules were forty-two cases of ·303 ammunition—approximately forty-two thousand rounds, and a welcome addition to my arsenal.

Thereafter, we directed our fire upon the company, and bereft of their principal armament, they put up but a sorry resistance. Purposely, I spared the chief officer, as I wanted him to return to Kabul in disgrace. In order to save his own face he would tell a wondrous tale of the military might of Bacha.

His men dropped all around him from the fire of my men, and I, personally, gave him plenty to think about. I removed his turban, smashed the hilt of his sword, and punctured his water-bottle, for now I could afford to play with ammunition, and I wanted a little amusement. Besides, it was but right that the poor man should have evidence of his valour. How it would assist him when he told Kabul of the great fight he put up!

I will be kind. All I will say is that eventually the Kabuli force retired. It was wise, for we could have picked off the remnant at any moment we desired.

As it was, we took the rifles of the slain, disposed of the wounded, and returned with our machine-guns and a goodly supply of ammunition.

Kabul made one more effort to impose its authority, and then it gave me best.

The infantry having failed, it decided to pitch the air force against me, and for days two aeroplanes winged their way over the tribal lands searching for Bacha's encampment.

At that time, however, I was on a tour of my domain, and it was my custom to stop at a different village every night, so that the unfortunate pilots must have thought they were looking for a scorpion in a field of corn.

Their patience, however, was exemplary, and they deserved a better fate than that which I accorded them.

Amongst the men who flocked to my banner at this time was one whom I viewed with a certain suspicion, and in order the better to keep an eye on him, I placed him among my own bodyguard. One afternoon, when we had reached a village where the immediate terrain was flat—the villagers were lucky in that they had a few fields at which they could scratch—I saw this man behave strangely. He unwound his turban, and placed it on the ground in the form of an elongated cross, and—the stem of the cross pointed to the village.

It was an action which might have passed if I had not my suspicions, for the man might easily have just washed his turban, but—I had spent some years in Peshawar, and I had seen British troops signal to aeroplanes by placing panels on the ground.

Later, when the two aeroplanes flew overhead, my suspicions were confirmed.

I said nothing at the time, but that night, when the time had come for rest, I said casually to one of my bodyguard:

"Abdul, bring me the red fruit of a cactus."

Wonderingly, the man rose to obey. He might well be puzzled, for the cactus fruit is covered with spikes, and the interior is a mass of small hair-like pricks. It is no delicacy, and even the donkeys will disdain it.

However, I held my men in converse around the fast falling fire, and waited for Abdul to return. He did so at length, holding the fruit gingerly.

Leaning lazily against my saddle, I called two of my men close towards me, and whispered,

"The newcomer," I said. "Seize him."

Without a word, the man was held, and disarmed.

"Open his mouth," I ordered, and fingers pressed on to his jaw bones until he gaped.

Popping the cactus fruit into his mouth, and pressing the point of my knife against his breast, I bade him eat. His eyes, alight with fury and distaste, bored into mine, but—he ate.

I knew that by the morrow his tongue would be swollen to the roof of his mouth, and that his cheeks, pricked on the inside by those tiny, poisonous irritants, would be so puffed that his face would be unrecognisable.

But, I had not finished.

I bade him remove his clothes, and under the menace of my knife, he did so. Then I disrobed, and I forced him to don my rather distinctive garments.

I salaamed to him ironically, and I bowed low in mock deference.

"I see before me Bacha Saquo," I said tauntingly. "Good, the great man shall have of the best. He shall rest upon Bacha's bed, for that is but right. And he shall have a bodyguard to see that evil does not befall him."

It was my well-known custom to have my charpoi well in the open, for I distrusted the shadows cast by walls, and around me the sentries of my bodyguard.

I had my charpoi carried out, and this man, attired in my clothes, was forced to lie upon it. The sentries were non-evident, but they were there all the same, and this man knew it.

I gave them orders to take up positions behind walls and the like, and to shoot the man dead if he made any attempt to move from my bed.

Nothing happened that night, but with the dawn, there came a whirring in the sky, and I laughed in my hand, for my surmise had been right. Lower and lower came the two aeroplanes, and suddenly they alighted on this heaven-sent stretch of flat ground. Figures jumped from the machines and ran with the speed of hares for the village.

They entered, and they had evidently been well primed, for they made straight for my charpoi, and threw themselves upon the prone figure there. They acted entirely without ceremony, and I grinned as I watched from a nearby hiding place while they seized this man by the hair and made play with his windpipe.

I could see his eyes entreating, and I could hear the "Blah, blah, blah," that came from his swollen mouth, and I stuffed the end of my turban in my quivering lips to stifle my laughter.

To add colour to the scene, I ordered one of our machine-guns to open out, and the aeroplanes replied, but the marksmen there were rather hampered in their work, as they could not spray the village at their pleasure. Their friends were inside, and had yet to emerge.

I saw the raiders seize upon my swollen-faced double, and hoist him up. Then, with a lurching run, they carried him off, making for the aeroplanes.

As soon as the ridiculous procession was clear, the second machine, given a field of fire, started up with its machine-gun to give supporting fire, but machine-gun or not, I could not restrain the impulse.

My double, slung across a man's back, kept giving frightened glances behind him, as if he expected the worst. I was determined that he should not be disappointed. Giving a scream like a dervish, and drawing my knife, I rushed in pursuit, and that man's eyes, as he was carried on helplessly, were a picture to be remembered. They goggled fright, and his wildly uttered "blahs" to his own comrades only added to the piquancy of an intriguing situation.

Waving my knife, and prancing wildly in an absurd burlesque of an avenger, I came up to the retreating figures, and—struck.

The blow was nicely timed, and I doubt whether it even pierced this fellow's skin. It did, however, dispose of his pyjama cord, and I gave a tug. The garments were mine, anyway.

I often wondered what they said to this spy in Kabul after they landed him there. It was probably two days before he could speak coherently, and quite that time before his face became recognisable.

I was left in peace after that.

I think the pyjamas did it.

CHAPTER IX

THE stars in their courses were shaping my destiny.

My shock tactics with the merchants, had made me master of the caravan routes. My manner of disposing of Sharfuddin, my principal, and therefore my only rival, made me paramount in the hills. The easy and blasé manner in which I had foiled the feeble attempts of the Kabul Government to bring me to heel, consolidated my position, and placed me definitely above all others in the province of Kohistan. There, my name meant the law. If Bacha said so, then it was so, and there was none to give me even the semblance of opposition. The people flew to my bidding. Those that were sprightly received their due reward. Those who were tardy were apt to find me churlish.

Such is the way of the hills. There can be no half measures.

I was Lord of Kohistan, and ruler of the caravans, and my name was known throughout Afghanistan. I could, in necessity, command a fighting force of great number, for practically the entire male population of my province was conscript at my word, and —I flatter myself there was more than fear that impelled the unhesitating obedience which I could conjure. The people were glad, and proud even, to bask in the reflected glory which was shed by the name and person of Bacha Saquo.

Glory? . . . Yes.

I was overlord—a personage of power, and—yes, of some dignity, for Bacha Saquo, though others pretended to forget, could never entirely eradicate from his mind that he was the son of the water-carrier.

And, in pretending to forget, and in doing me honour, I knew that these others did but pretend. I was not to be fooled by power and circumstance. I was no mere hillman who had jumped to an eminence from his own village fire. I had travelled, and I had seen. I had beheld the fawning, genu-flecting mob that surrounded the court at Kabul, and I had seen them bending the knee, and—I had heard of their private converse. Such matters can come as a revelation, and I had no false illusions regarding the perfidy of man.

No, when persons came to accord me honour, I subconsciously stripped these praise-singers of their urbane exterior, and I sought that which was in the mind behind those smiling, unctuous eyes. Seldom did I fail to discern the cess-pool of gain and jealousy, of avarice and cynicism. This analysis, to which all were secretly subjected, did much to keep me within the realm of fact and substance. Always had I both feet firmly planted on reality. Never did I allow my fancy to secure possession of my body, and to whirl me away into the fantastic spheres of improbability and vainglory.

I realised that to enhance and sustain my posi-tion, I must not rest on my laurels. Moreover, I

could not continue indefinitely as a mere robber of
the trade routes. True, I had my amulet, but the
way of the assassin's knife is sure, and there are
ever those in the robber's band whose fingers tingle
to perform that one, short, sharp stroke which will
give them the leadership.

No, I must needs do more than that. The
merchants were met when their caravans were
entering the hills, and they were required to pay
for safe custody. To those who demurred it was
pointed out that the payment of a levy at that
stage was preferable to the entire loss of one's goods
in the passes. And, when it was delicately hinted
that attaching to the lost goods there would be
the owner's life, these merchants saw the light of
day, and—paid.

When they paid, they were guaranteed safe
custody, and my power over the hillmen was sufficient to ensure this. Those who went awry of my
will, and demonstrated a penchant for the recalcitrant, were certain of elevation.

At strategic points among the hills I had tall
posts erected, and attached to these posts were
wooden cages. Those who merited my displeasure
were provided with free lodging in these airy confines,
and were hoisted upward.

Devoid of food and drink it was amazing how
long these hardy people took to die, but—the trade
routes were guaranteed.

Naturally, my levying of taxes was not looked
upon with any transports of pleasure by those in
receipt of custom in Kabul. On arrival there the
merchants would protest that they had already been

heavily mulcted, and could pay no more. This was a serious matter for the Treasury, and especially for the customs officials who battened thereon, and loud were the cries of rage and anguish which went up from Kabul against the rapacious Bacha.

But Bacha saw means whereby he could further consolidate his position.

He took pity on the Kabul Government, and thereafter the levy on the merchants was increased. Bacha had a power over the caravans which the Government lacked. He could say: "Pay, or there is death in the passes." And, of course, the merchants paid.

The amount of the extra levy I transmitted to Kabul with an ironically gracious letter in which I left the court in no doubt as to the extent of my bounty. Kabul, naturally, perhaps, in the circumstances, affected to ignore me, but—it did not return the money.

Thus, in a measure, I secured recognition in the capital. Certainly, the whole countryside chuckled, and there were even those at the court who cast envious glances upon the hills in the direction of one who could afford to be magnanimous, and give the Government of his charity.

Oh, yes. It was an astute move.

This was no pandering to man's innate vanity. In adopting this course I had a greater issue at stake. Naturally, the power to be able to embarrass the arrogant Kabulis gave me pleasure, but there was a certain method in my seeming madness.

Sitting up there in the hills of Kohistan, I was in a better position to read the portents than those who were immersed in the vortex. There was much that the King was doing wrong. Gradually, he was moving to the pass where there would be a struggle of wills, and—long ago I had come to the conclusion that Amanullah Khan was both a bluffer and a blunderer. I was biding my time, and sowing the seed.

Moreover, he was one who went back on his plighted word, and—no ruler of Afghanistan can afford to do that.

When there arose the insurrection in Khost, Amanullah promised the chieftains that his ill-favoured new laws would be withdrawn. They were, but—only to be reimposed when all was at peace again.

When the time came to revert to his scheme of reformation, Amanullah committed a cardinal error in his efforts to placate the tribesmen. He informed the chiefs, with a wealth of verbiage, that they were God's children and that the only people who had resisted the reforms in the first instance were the Mullahs. He thereupon addressed himself to the task of hounding the clergy—easily the most powerful and most numerous individual class within his domain. The priests, he said, were the barriers to real progress. Therefore, the priests must bend the knee, or go.

He hit at time-honoured customs and tradition, and the people began to murmur, and asked if their King had become afflicted in his mind. Not only did they hesitate to obey the Royal commands, but it was the invariable custom to refer these matters to the Mullahs. The advice tendered by the priests frequently ran counter to the Royal *firman*.

Amanullah was determined that the women of Afghanistan should forgo the veil. All women were ordered to show their faces, and his favourites were those men who ordered their womenfolk to plaster their skin with European cosmetics, and to array their bodies in the latest confections from Paris.

According to ancient custom, women only had their hair shorn if they were disgraced, but Amanullah thought that all should cut their hair, in imitation of the women of the West. Also, he decreed that the ancient tradition of regarding Friday as a holiday and a holy day in fact, should be abandoned, and that the Moslem holiday should be on Thursdays.

His most fantastic order was that the people should desert their ancient garb, and resort to European clothes. He actually gave orders that only those attired in European raiment should be admitted to certain parks and thoroughfares.

He decreed also that students should not marry, and that his army should have no relations with the Mullahs.

Also, the ancient methods of recruitment for the army were abandoned, and a system of ballot substituted.

This latter gave cause of much heartburning to another very powerful class. Under what was known as the Qomi system, every clan was required to furnish a certain number of men for the army according to its numerical strength. This was subsequently changed so that every eighth man was called up, and then Amanullah Khan conceived the idea of ballot. In some countries such a form of recruitment might work, but it could not spell anything but trouble and corruption under an administration such as then obtained in Afghanistan.

The new system was known as "Pishk." A family had only to quarrel with one who conducted the lotteries, and the next day perhaps the only son was informed that the ballot had selected him for the army. To many of the more powerful families, service in the lower ranks, which perforce included a number of menial tasks, was highly repugnant, and for these there was a "buying-out" safety valve, the usual sum being fifteen hundred Kaldar rupees (£100). It was perhaps only in the nature of things that this buying-out process should have been fairly constant. The way of the ballot pointed to those with money with amazing regularity, and the recruiting officers were soon some of the richest in the land. Later, I made a point of seeking out Amanullah's ballot keepers, but that is by the way.

Thus, the months passed in growing discontent. The King was squeezing all for taxes with which to pay for his new and hated reforms. In Hind, they were building a great new capital. It was even said that in far off Australia where men sometimes went as camel drivers, they were doing the same. What Hind and Australia could do, Amanullah Khan could do. He commenced to spend crores of rupees upon bricks and mortar a short distance from Kabul. Amanullah also would have a great city which would bear his name, and keep his memory green in the minds of posterity.

In an atmosphere definitely antagonistic to the Throne, Amanullah decided upon his great "European pilgrimage." Had he known of the great weight of feeling against him, he would have hesitated in leaving his kingdom at such a time, but he was fully under the impression that the people welcomed his reforms, and that the only persons with whom he had to contend were the Mullahs. His courtiers told him this, and none others were allowed to approach the Royal presence. So satisfied was the King that his policy was right that his principal amusement was to hale a bearded Mullah before him, and then deride him for his bearded face and his comical garments. The courtiers, in their creased trousers from London, and their faultless morning coats, would preen themselves, laugh with the King, and thus spend a pleasant hour.

Wild tales of these entertainments would make their way to the hills, and there was much reflective tugging of beards.

In order to secure funds for the King's going, the Treasury had to embark upon perilous schemes. The host of reforms which Amanullah Khan had initiated had eaten up the taxes as fast as they were garnered, and when the King asked for his fare to Europe there was much scratching of heads.

Eventually it was decided to mulct the wealthy who were required to provide "voluntary" contributions to this great Affair of State, and for the rest, to levy three years' taxes in advance on the remainder of the population with, of course, the notable exception of Kohistan where, if there was

any tax-gathering, Bacha Saquo did it quite
expeditiously.

The consternation of the people when suddenly
confronted with a demand for three years' taxes
can be imagined. No one is enamoured of the tax-
gatherer at any time, but in such circumstances——

In some cases the taxmen were fortunate. In
others, notwithstanding the machinery which was
implemented to squeeze the last drop from the
stone, not more than a year's taxation in advance
was procurable. There comes a time when even
the expert in extortion has to confess himself at
a loss.

Amanullah departed, and while he was absent
seeing of the wonders of the West at first hand,
there was much apprehensive speculation in Afghanistan as to the outcome. But I, Bacha, sitting up
in his hills like a vulture waiting for the living
thing to become a corpse, could afford to display
patience. A mentality such as that of Amanullah's
demanded an inexhaustible supply of money. Already he had wrung the country dry. Extortion
is a two-handed jade, and I could visualise the time
when this spendthrift monarch would be left suspended with a poverty stricken and hostile people
on the one hand, and a series of half consummated
reforms on the other.

For Amanullah there was not to be the fruit of
attainment—only the dry husk of frustrated
endeavour.

However, the hill vulture did make one or two
preliminary flights during the King's absence, during
which contact was made with Mohamed Wali,

Amanullah's favourite, and to whom he had dedicated the regency.

Mohamed Wali was making the most of his opportunities as one should in such circumstances, and I was anxious to spy out the land, for in certain eventualities, knowledge would mean power.

Mohamed Wali had no illusions about the future, hence his wholehearted endeavours to deplete the Treasury and when, by devious means, I met him, his reception was not that which should be accorded an enemy of the State. Rather did he appear anxious to temporise, as if he would guarantee that in the time to come there could not be brought against him any charge of obduracy. Indeed, the Vazir might even have been friendly, but in truth, he was such a poor liar that I despised him. An Afghan may admire one who can avoid the truth with grace and agility. He recognises this as one of the fine arts, but the gauche bungler merely excites his sympathy or his ire. I regarded Mohamed Wali as a time server with but one attribute. That was an unswerving devotion to his own person. He was resolved, no matter what happened to the rest of Afghanistan, that he at least would not go hungry, and might perchance become a King himself.

On two occasions I saw this man, it being given out in Kabul that he had opened pourparlers with Bacha Saquo because the latter desired to submit to the Government. The rascal said that in order to save his face. Actually, there was no whisper of my submission, and the Vazir knew it. Mohamed Wali was looking into the distance, and was taking no chances.

That which I saw in Kabul during these visits made it evident to me that I had only to wait a favourable opportunity. I was certain that time was on my side, and events were to prove that I was not wrong in my prognostication.

Summed up, I merely had to retire to my hills and allow another to open the gates of Kabul to me.

Amanullah Khan returned from his travels, his mind aflame with what he had seen in the West, and—the train was set.

CHAPTER X

I SOUND THE TOCSIN

In the autumn of 1928 Amanullah Khan returned to Kabul via Persia and Herat. Throughout her travels, Queen Suraya had gone unveiled, and she was attired in the most expensive raiment of the West. At the court of the Shah, a request was made to King Amanullah that his consort should resume the veil. This in itself should have been an indication to Amanullah of the temper of his own people in respect to this ancient matter of custom. But, no. Amanullah Khan was resolved to bring his country in line with the progressives. In Egypt the veil had been largely discarded, and in Turkey, under the Ghazi, women were galloping toward emancipation. But, Turkey is Turkey, and Egypt is Egypt and Afghanistan is a law unto itself. What changes there are must come slowly, and with the will of the people.

Between Kabul and Kohistan I had a line of trusty runners. There were those within the court circle who would do anything for money, and I, Bacha Saquo, could afford to buy my information. Also, I had means of testing its accuracy. I did not rely upon one single channel, but had several, and I was thus enabled to sift the chaff from the wheat and arrive at a mean which was near enough fact for my purpose.

Before forty-eight hours had passed after Amanullah's return, my runners were pouring astonishing tales in my ears. Some were so strange that they were difficult of acceptance, yet there was abundant proof that they were true. Were not the *dursies* of Kabul working day and night with their needles, and were not the second-hand clothes merchants of Hind pouring bale after bale of Ferenghi rubbish across the border?

The Royal *firman* was that the face of Afghanistan must be changed. Amanullah Khan saw in our flowing pyjamas and embroidered waistcoats only that which was repugnant. He would have all, from the highest to the lowest, in European garb. He had returned from the West with the silk-hat complex, and he thought more of the correct position for a trouser crease and of the shine to his patent leather shoes than he did of the dignity of his countrymen.

Here was his second cardinal blunder. He decreed that his countrymen should sacrifice their dignity and make themselves ridiculous—and that is something to which no true-born will submit with equanimity.

But there was the order. Everyone must wear European dress, and women had to go unveiled. The net result was every peasant cursed his King, and a journey to Kabul was regarded as a penance only to be undertaken if absolutely imperative.

On the outskirts of the city there grew up a strange trade. Pedlars with European garments hired out their wares by the hour and by the day in order that those who had business in the city might appear in the hated garb and thus get by the police.

The occasion was one for ribaldry and jest, and —for curses. Stalwart peasants, who had never as much as seen a white man, were waylaid on their way to Kabul by these harpies, and informed that they could not appear on the streets unless they crowned their heads with a battered bowler, draped their arms through a bedraggled coat, and thrust their legs through misfit trousers. In some circumstances the effect might have been laughable, but there was always the reflection: There, but for the grace of Allah, go I—and the laughter was restrained and all one heard were curses upon the monarch who would do this thing to his people.

Such stories, and more came to me, and—with the stories a growing infiltration of men from Amanullah's army. I, Bacha Saquo, at this time had money and to spare. The levy I obtained from the caravans was not expended on exotic frivolities, and those whom I received beneath my banner could be certain of their just dues. But, there was a far different tale to tell in Kabul and in Jalalabad. For many months the army had hungered for its pay, and the twenty rupees per mensum had proved to be little more than a promise. The men who came to me were in uniform, it is true, but it was uniform which badly needed attention, and more often than not, complete renewal.

These deserters told me extraordinary tales of the disruption within the army ranks. The officers, too, were affected, for with the sepoys not receiving their pay, how were the higher ranks to exact their commissions?

The time I now knew was rapidly approaching —the time when I must put my trust in the Mullah's prophecy.

There were murmurings among the people; the army was disgruntled, and a rebellious clergy was stalking the land impressing upon the peasants that they were in the hands of Satan. The court was reviled; Amanullah was likened to a madman; tax-gatherers who still endeavoured to mulct the poor were murdered, and there was a drying up of resources in Kabul. The King had spent all on his journeys abroad; the country had paid its taxes long in advance, and the State coffers were running empty.

Each day, sitting up in the hills, I awaited the call which I knew must come. And, I was prepared. I was sanguine of victory, too, for my star was definitely in the ascendant. The one Afghan soldier for whom I had any regard, and the one commander whom I did not despise, was in Europe, seriously ill: he was General Nadir Khan who was away, and beyond easy recall. It required but a master stroke, and I would call Amanullah Khan's bluff.

I sat up in the hills scanning the horizon for the cloud which would mark the advent of the great storm that was brewing. As with the way of the winds, that cloud hovered somewhere else, and well to the southward. Fate decreed that the storm should break well beyond the hills, and that my path to the city of Kabul be rendered the more easy.

In times such as these, when a whole country is on the tip-toe of expectation; when every man fears to go to bed because of what the morrow might bring, news travels quickly.

The air was electrified, and all that was required was a spark. The spark fell in unexpected territory.

A party of Koochi tribesmen were passing through the Shinwari country. It had with it merchandise of considerable value, and was apprehensive of attack. Coming upon some armed Shinwaris it mistook the locals for brigands on the pillage, and shots were exchanged. A number of Shinwari casualties spoke to the character of the engagement, and the tribesmen were furious. They rose throughout the countryside and fell upon and captured the Koochis, and hauled them before the local magistrate.

This was a small thing, and an insignificant incident in a land such as Afghanistan, and anyone searching for the spark would have passed it by, and looked elsewhere.

But, such is the way of life, this magistrate had failed to receive his salary for a considerable period, and he had reached that pass when justice must needs give place to expediency.

The Koochis were men of substance. They had with them considerable wealth. What was more natural that they should disgorge, and go free? It was said that they parted with ten thousand rupees to save their necks.

Whatever the amount, and whatever went on behind the scenes, these Koochis were well on their way by morning, and the Shinwaris believed that they had been robbed of justice.

All this came to me as a whisper—as a matter of passing interest, and of no moment. Even so, it was the prelude to a revolution, and the beginning of the end for Amanullah.

The Shinwaris, already tax-burdened, already at variance with their King, already convinced that their wrongs were many, took this slight by the magistrate as the last straw, and they assembled around his house, calling loudly for him to appear that they might slay him.

Being a magistrate, he defied the mob and was able to call upon the local police for protection, but the Shinwaris still wanted his blood. Village after village rose and banded together to increase the clamour, and soon thousands had joined together in armed lashkars and were looking for trouble. Amanullah sent various officers to the Shinwari country to impress upon the people the wrong they were committing in resorting to arms, and the officers were either flung into prison or so maltreated that they were glad to escape and return to Kabul with their lives.

Eventually, the magistrate who was the cause of all the disturbance, was taken by the Shinwaris. He was soundly thrashed in public; other indignities were poured upon him, and he was flung into jail.

Now came the crucial moment. Having attained their immediate object, and having the magistrate at their mercy, would the Shinwaris declare themselves satisfied and disperse to their homes?

Away up in the hills of Kohistan there was one who awaited news with the greatest anxiety. The torch of revolt had been lighted. Now, would it fizzle out?

It seemed that it would.

A large and influential jirgah was summoned at which the Shinwari clan leaders discussed the matter.

The officer who had disgraced them had been punished and imprisoned. Was it necessary, then, to remain at arms?

There were two views expounded. There were those, by no means in the minority, who declared that honour had been satisfied. There were those, however, who said with some truth, that they had satisfied their honour, but at the expense of the King's. The standard of revolt had been raised, they explained. The King's officers had been abused and maltreated, and these men, having the ear of the King, trouble was bound to ensue.

This point was so poignant, and so easy of assimilation, that it won the jirgah. From there, the scope of the discussion was enlarged, until it came to a discourse not on peace or war, but how best to maintain the Shinwaris in arms in order to obtain redress from the ruler.

Throughout the night, speaker followed speaker, and it was eventually decided that Amanullah had betrayed his trust and should be thrust from the throne. It was declared also that Queen Suraya, who had bared her face to the multitude, should be expelled from the country, together with all her relations, particularly the King's father-in-law, Mahmud Tarzi, whom some held in abhorrence because of his ways and his mode of living.

The Mullahs, whom the King affected to despise,

were there at the jirgah giving of their spiritual advice. It did not tend to soften the feelings of the Shinwaris toward the court at Kabul.

When that jirgah broke up, Shinwari deputations were already on their way throughout the tribal lands to induce other clans to join the revolt for the freeing of the country.

War was in the air. The vulture, sitting up on his hilltop, fluttered his wings, but did not immediately make for the killing. Bacha Saquo would allow this movement to obtain impetus and then he would strike.

I did not have to wait long. Amanullah was to play right into my hands.

First of all he sought to quell the Shinwari revolt by inciting other tribes to rise against the rebels. He poured out arms and ammunition and arrayed the Lugmanis, the Chaparharis and other tribes against the Shinwaris, but except to accept his arms and his ammunition these tribesmen showed a distinct reluctance to fight against their neighbours. Actually, the court blundered in believing that money and arms would buy over these men at such a time. It failed utterly to realise how great was the resentment everywhere obtaining against the King and all his ways.

News was brought to me of the tribes rising everywhere in the south and in the east. The country became so disturbed that the Khyber caravan rout had to be closed. Then, the rebels attacked Kahi, and ransacked the armoury there and retired from the scene well armed. It was but a step from there to the capture of Jalalabad, and Amanullah poured out his troops from Kabul in an effort to confront the menace.

From Jalalabad came further and graver news. The rebels evolved twenty-one points, among them being the resignation of the King, the non-acceptance of any of his house as the future ruler, the dismissal of the Queen and her relations, the desposition of all the Ministers, and a complete reversal of all new laws.

When he received this ultimatum Amanullah despatched yet further forces to the east, and the vulture again gave a preliminary flutter of his wings.

Then came word that the rebels had decided to march on Kabul.

I, Bacha Saquo, determined to be there first.

In my province of Kohistan there was still a man who was Governor in name. Hitherto I had pretended to ignore this person's existence for he caused me no let or hindrance, and indeed, was the most inoffensive of men. I will not say that he was incompetent, because I do not know how otherwise he could have countered the situation with which he was presented. Rather would I say that he was a wise man who allowed little to trouble him—not even the frequent and peremptory demands he received from Kabul to arrest and imprison that bumptious brigand, Bacha Saquo.

Now that the time had come, however, the standard of revolt had openly to be raised, and I could think of no better way of sounding the tocsin than embarrassing the man who stood for the Royal edict.

Gathering my bodyguard, I proceeded across the hills to this person's residence. Quickly, the place was surrounded.

Alone, I stepped into the great one's room. He was sipping his green tea. I covered him with my revolvers, and tied him to the legs of his iron safe. It was an undignified stance for a Governor, but he had been an inoffensive man who had done me no hurt, and I did not desire his blood.

I stalked over to the telephone which gave on to a private line direct to the capital.

"Give me the palace," I cried.

"Yes—yes—the Governor speaking. . . . Quickly —the King's own personal number. . . ."

A voice such as I had heard many times came crackling over the wire. Its cadences were unmistakable. It was the King.

"I have the honour to report to Your Majesty," I said, "that I have captured the brigand, Bacha Saquo. What would Your Majesty have done with him?"

His Majesty did not hesitate. The reply came back harshly and imperiously.

"Shoot the scoundrel like the dog that he is!"

Amanullah hung up the telephone.

I laughed loud and long in my beard.

With all his attentions directed toward the east, the King would give no thought to a brigand-chief whom he believed to be dead.

The vulture of the hills was ready to strike.

Before morning two thousand well armed men had answered my summons.

I mustered them, and surveyed them appraisingly.

Every man was a fighter, and every man had been well paid and knew that he could follow Bacha Saquo with confidence.

It was enough.

"Advance!"

I had taken my first active step to the throne.

CHAPTER XI

THE FIRST PHASE

I KNEW that Amanullah Khan was a braggart; I knew that he was a bluffer, and I knew that he was a fool so utterly to give himself over to the place-seekers by whom he was surrounded. Yet, Bacha Saquo, who prided himself on his native perspicacity, was not the astute appraiser of men that he imagined himself to be. I made a profound error in my earlier calculations which might easily have cost me dear. I under-estimated the heights to which Amanullah's arrogance could carry him. I did him an injustice. I believed that in the face of profound danger he would act as would other men. That he did not I was only to learn subsequently, but the belief that the King's actions would be guided by common-sense did much to circumscribe my actions when first I extended my hand for the throne.

When first the Shinwari tribesmen raised the banner of revolt, there was acute apprehension in Kabul as to what I, Bacha, the brigand-chief, would do.

Through the Governor of Kohistan, certain overtures were made to me which I did not take very seriously. It was suggested to me that in return for sundry considerations I should surrender my overlordship of the caravan routes, and I replied, more

in satire than anything else, that I would consent
to this course if I were guaranteed personal protection, were given an adequate sum of money to meet
my needs, one hundred ·303 rifles, and two thousand
rounds of ammunition for each weapon. I hinted
that in return, I would disband many of my men
and send them to Kabul as recruits to the forces
which would operate against the rebel Shinwaris.

When, in addition to my terms, I demanded some
form of military title I did not think for one moment
that the court would entertain my suggestion, but
to my surprise, and no little delight, it did.

The Governor used his telephone to some purpose,
the money and the rifles and ammunition arrived,
and I was told that the question of military rank
was only one for discussion and mutual arrangement.

I could not have been provided with a more
acceptable present.

In accordance with my promise I despatched a
number of men to Kabul. All were retained in my
pay, and all had orders to incite the Shinwaris to
further rebellion rather than fight against them,
and to spread the fame of the name of Bacha
Saquo.

Altogether, therefore, I could muster some two
hundred and fifty ·303 rifles of accepted make, some
fifty ·303 weapons of tribal manufacture, two
machine-guns and perhaps eighty thousand rounds
of ammunition. For the rest my force was armed
with ancient muzzle-loaders of doubtful potency—
good enough for work in the hills, but lacking in
precision and rapidity of action for the task I had
in mind.

I, too, had to proceed warily. When actually in the foothills which led from my mountains to Kabul I could count on the active sympathies of the villagers. They, because of their daily intercourse with the capital, had felt the full weight of Amanullah's laws. They, more than anyone else, had to participate in the senseless burlesques with European attire, and they were bitter against the King. Also, they were there *in situ* for the squeezing talons of the tax-collectors, and they sat in their villages and sighed. They looked across the ranges which divided them from Bacha Saquo, and thought of the plenty in money and victuals which was associated with his name.

There, all was well, but between the foothills and my sphere of action there was a belt of tribal land too near the capital to come under my dominance. Here there were a number of powerful Elders who had perforce to bend the knee to the dictates of Kabul. Here, there was danger.

I could not afford to descend with my entire force and initiate a battle for possession of Kabul. The place was a citadel, it was protected by many cannon, and it invariably housed an adequate garrison. If I descended in force, and there was a protracted siege, I should have a numerous and efficient enemy at my back. That could not be.

True, Amanullah believed me to be dead, but no large force could penetrate this hostile belt without news preceding it, and putting the capital on its guard.

Also, I was always a firm believer in possessing an adequate reserve—a force which a commander could throw into the breach when that moment came when a battle was to be won or lost.

I decided, therefore, that my initial descent upon the capital should be undertaken by the three hundred possessing modern rifles. The remaining seventeen hundred I would march up to the belt of hostile territory to be ready for emergencies.

I evolved a series of smoke and fire signals. This large force had to be ready, to march to my aid if I so requested, to move to a flank and create a diversion if I required a corridor through the hostile tract through which I could retire with speed and without fighting and at all times to make its presence felt by continual movement and desultory sniping. In other words, it was to prowl. It was too large to be lightly attacked. Always was it to expose a belligerent exterior. Always was it to be a menace.

It was near enough to Kabul to create uneasiness and alarm, and word had frequently to go out that I, Bacha, was in personal command.

Thus it was that I set out on my great adventure. My main body halted as I had planned and advertised its presence to some purpose. I, with my three hundred men, slipped through the hostile tract, and split up within the villages near Kabul. There, not only could I wait, but I could see.

Even as I marched, events were proceeding apace. The revolt of the Shinwaris was growing in momentum. There had been a battle of sorts at Nimla on the road to Kabul, and the Royalist troops had been routed. The way from the east to the capital was open. In the south the men of Badakshan were in arms, and were as one with the Shinwaris, and then news came that the conflagration had reached the western province of Herat.

In disguise I made several lone sorties into Kabul, and I could sense the strain in the atmosphere. I sent word to my main body to make yet more noise. They complied with gusto, and Kabul trembled lest I, who was already within its walls, should descend from the hills and sack it.

There were continuous conferences in the palace, and the courtiers went to and fro day and night. It was said in court circles that if only the King could dispose of this man, Bacha Saquo, all would still be well, and it was decided to send a force into the hills to encompass his defeat.

One Ahmed Ali Khan, who had just returned from a four years' sojourn in Berlin, was named as my executioner, and with an adequate force he set out for the hills. My men were apprised of his coming even before he knew he had been given this dubious command, for—I had my own methods of obtaining my information. Mohamed Wali, the King's Vazir, still kept his money bags open that those who cared might contribute.

Perhaps in order to show how well we understood one another Mohamed Wali presented me with a richly chased rifle. It had automatic action and I was to prove its efficiency in battle. Also—it was a beautiful adjunct to the durbar.

This be as it may, Ahmed Ali Khan proceeded with his force to the tract which I have termed hostile to me, and there sought counsel of the Elders. He called together a large jirgah at which all the principal men were present, and for two days and two nights he reiterated one thing:

Bacha Saquo must die.

The Elders had no reason to bear me any love, and eventually Ahmed Ali Khan's words sank home. The Elders were asked to raise all their able-bodied men—they estimated that they could arm six thousand—and to dispose of the force which was creating such a clamour on their borders. Also, they were requested to despatch several hundred men to Kabul to augment its garrison and to fight the Shinwaris.

At the end of the second night Ahmed Ali Khan slightly altered his tune. He proposed three expedients.

For a reward of one lakh of rupees (less than £10,000) the Elders were to encompass my death, dispose of my men, and carry my severed head to Kabul.

For a lesser reward, the Elders were to take to arms and segregate my men from the rest of the highland peasantry and to confine me to an area from which I could not escape.

For an even lesser reward they were to induce Bacha Saquo to surrender on terms, on the Government's guarantee of security.

In the end the Elders decided that they would raise their six thousand men as an inducement to me to surrender and close with the third of the proposals, securing in the meantime from Kabul a guarantee for my personal safety.

The terms were drawn up, and as is our custom, were placed upon two Holy Qurans. On the document a space was left for the signature of Amanullah which would accord me a full pardon.

The two volumes of the Holy Book, and the document, were forwarded to Kabul, and the Elders waited.

I, of course, had not the slightest intention that this document should ever receive the King's signature, and I took steps accordingly. Bacha Saquo was not going to have it said that he received clemency from the hands of this man, and then violated that which had been rendered inviolable on the Holy Quran.

When the Holy Books were taken into the King's apartment at the palace, he from whose head the crown was even then slipping would have had a heart attack could he have seen behind the rich draperies which diffused the light from one of the great windows. That he, the King, should be harbouring in his own holy of holies the very man for whose life he was prepared to pay almost any amount in money and dignity, did not occur to him, and it was not for Bacha Saquo to enlighten him.

Then and there I could have disposed of Amanullah, notwithstanding the promise I had given Mohamed Wali, but the urge was not in me. I knew this man to be of clay, and I believed that if he were sufficiently hard pressed, he would break, and—flee. Were he to die by the hand of the assassin, or were he to die gloriously in battle, there would be a halo attaching to his name, and the country would look to his son as the rightful heir. But, no Afghan will forgive a man who runs, and—I wanted Amanullah Khan to run.

Mohamed Wali entered the Royal apartment, the two Holy Books carried carefully and decorously on his open palms. He bowed low to Amanullah, who growled. For many nights the King had been without proper sleep, and he was showing the strain. There were deep lines in his olive, full-fleshed face, and as he sat he gave repeated, nervous hitches to the European trousers which encased his legs like Ferenghi drain pipes. Occasionally he would raise a hand to his tousled hair, and there was a tell-tale tremor to his fingers.

Looking upon Amanullah then I could see two great forces at variance. There was the dreaminess of the reformer hitched to a sullen obstinacy which was almost that of the schoolboy. There was the protruding under lip, drooping at the sides, which betokened sulkiness and moroseness, and a spasmodic outjutting of the chin which indicated the contumacious and the self-opinionated.

But, the tired eyes were sombre and dismal. They were heavy with dire foreboding, and they told of the fight even then being waged between the two characteristics of this King.

"Well," growled Amanullah. "Another petition?"
The Vazir grovelled.

"Your Majesty," he replied, "it is an agreement which has been drawn up between Ahmed Ali Khan and the Elders of Kohistan. . . ."

"Yes, yes?" Amanullah was impatient.

"It is suggested, Your Majesty, that in return for an unconditional pardon, Bacha Saquo, the low-born brigand, will surrender."

"Oh!" Amanullah reached forward, and picked up a pen.

"Your Majesty." Mohamed Wali spoke softly,

yet tensely. "Should the King sign an agreement
with a low-born who has heaped so much indignity
upon the Royal house?"

Amanullah's hand wavered, and he gazed at the
document upon the Koran with distaste.

"You are right, Mohamed Wali," he muttered
testily. "Ahmed Ali Khan was despatched to bring
in this man's head, not his insolent demands."

"Let Ahmed Ali Khan sign it, Your Majesty!"
counselled Wali!

He flung the pen from him, and rose. He stalked
angrily from the room.

With a covert glance in the direction of the
window draperies the Vazir gathered up the books,
and retired.

By means known only to me and Mohamed Wali
I made my way from the palace, and collected my
three hundred stalwarts from the nearby villages.
Carefully, and moving only at night, I proceeded to
the place where Ahmed Ali Khan still tarried with
the Elders.

A few hours after my arrival those with the
Holy Koran appeared, and made their way to the
tribal fires, for it was winter and extremely cold,
and all huddled there in their sheepskin coats.

The deputation's spokesman was opening his
mouth when I stepped forward, a row of grinning
rifle muzzles at my back, and the astonishment of
Ahmed Ali Khan and of the Elders was worth
that moment. Dismay mingled with perturbation
in humorous extravaganza, for the flickering light
of the fires illumined all, and threw all countenances
into relief.

"So, Ahmed Ali Khan . . . you would give up Bacha to the King!"

There was ridicule and insult in my words, and the commander of the Government forces moved uneasily. I had pricked his self-esteem at the first stab, and I knew that I had him at a disadvantage. As for the Elders, they sat there, silently, pulling at their beards, philosophically waiting for what Bacha should bring them.

I glanced significantly at the Koran which was borne in the hands of the deputations' leader, and shook my head scoffingly.

"There were three men in the King's room," I jeered, when the Koran was presented for signature."

I laughed loud and long at this man's discomfiture.

"The third man," I said, "has told me that the King has not signed."

My tone was caustic.

I advanced a pace nearer the fires.

"And, Ahmed Ali Khan," I continued menacingly, "this third man tells me to be careful of thee!"

With a curse and a scramble, Ahmed Ali Khan was on his feet, and was beyond the fires and in their shadows. I withheld my riflemen, for I did not desire to slaughter the Elders of my own clan. I could not afford to antagonise them and to lose the support of my own countrymen.

But, leaving fifty of my men to warm themselves by the fires and not, as the Elders might suppose, to intimidate them, I rushed onward with the remaining two hundred and fifty and fell upon the encampment of the Royal troopers.

These parade ground men dislike the dark. They have been drilled to cope with an enemy that can be seen; not one that emerges from the shadows and sticks a bayonet in their vitals. It was not a great or glorious fight, and we lost but one man killed and two wounded before the Kabulis took to their heels. Both Ahmed Ali Khan and his brother escaped in the darkness and the confusion, which was as well. They could return to Kabul, and help to spread the terror of my name.

This small and insignificant encounter had a result which was to stand me in good stead, though I was to remain unaware of it for some days.

Ahmed Ali Khan returned to the palace to make his excuses to a highly incensed monarch. Instead of my head he had sent an insolent letter; instead of defeating me, he had himself been routed.

In vain he pleaded that the Kohistan Elders had been in league with me. In vain he pleaded that he was confronted by an overwhelming force. In vain he pleaded to be allowed to return with more soldiers to encompass my death, or die himself in battle. He was relieved of his command and disgraced.

But the words with which he had sought to excuse himself with the King bore fruit. The hundreds of tribesmen already despatched by the Elders for the defence of Kabul were regarded with suspicion. They were not served out with arms, and eventually they drifted back to their homes. Most of them finally enrolled themselves under my banner.

CHAPTER XII

I ATTACK KABUL

THE night after the rout of Ahmed Ali Khan I was back in the villages around Kabul. I thought I knew something of the man I would dispossess, and I was determined to avoid, if possible, circumstances where Amanullah would have no other recourse but to lead his men into battle.

There would come the moment, so I believed, when the country would have to say: Who shall be King?

Amanullah Khan must not only be dispossessed, but his name must be disgraced. Then, with no one ready to fill the breach, and with Bacha Saquo in command at Kabul, the clans would be the more likely to accept the situation.

I had no illusions. I knew that they would look askance at the son of a water-carrier, and that if any other aspirant to the throne lifted his head there would be war. But, if Amanullah could be induced to abdicate—if his nerves could be fretted to that degree when he lost his self-command, and with Nadir Khan sickly and ill in Europe, I stood to have what I could hold.

My initial move, therefore, was an attack which was not an attack. That night I ringed the city with my men, and we sniped unceasingly. There is nothing so intimidating; nothing so demoralising as a rain of well directed bullets from an enemy who is unseen; whose strength is a matter for fantastic guess-work, and whose reputation is one where one instinctively thinks of rivers of blood.

The residents of Kabul had no sleep that night, even though there were several quiet interludes. During one of these I actually entered the city— no difficult task in the rain and the icy wind—and I knew that I had the place at my mercy. I could have rushed the defences that night, but there would have been bloody work in the streets, and Amanullah would have been forced to fight. I desired to nag at this man's nerves, and not to antagonise the people of Kabul. Much would shortly depend upon their reactions to certain contingencies.

I continued the sniping throughout most of the next day, and made several feints in the open against the city. None of these, however, was pressed home. Their purpose was to keep the defenders up to concert pitch, and to add weight and force to the sniping.

During the day, also, I called down a number of my men from the hills. It was necessary to increase my force now that so much was visible. In all my men numbered now over one thousand. The three hundred men with modern arms I kept at their sniping. The others I utilised for the feint attacks on the city. Their weapons produced sufficient noise for an army, and, morally, did more damage than the modern rifle.

Kabul's defences were indeed in a sorry state, for Amanullah had thrown all his men south-eastward to meet the menace of the Shinwaris. Only the men of the King's bodyguard remained, and their efforts were augmented by the students of the Military College.

During the day emissaries arrived from the revolting Shinwaris, and I gave them free passage into the city. Word came to me that Amanullah refused to receive them that day. Eventually, however, he changed his mind, and did so.

These men brought with them the demands of the Shinwari jirgah which, at the outset did not call for the King's abdication. The Shinwaris, and the clans who had gathered to them, demanded the recall of the irritating new laws, and Amanullah agreed. Before the representatives of the rebels he would agree to anything, but before these men left the city they were vouchsafed an opportunity of gauging the worth to be placed upon his word.

As soon as these men had left the Royal presence, the courtiers were telling the King that the Mullahs were the real instigators of the revolt. Certainly, the hand of the Mullahs stood out strongly in the demands, and Amanullah fumed and raved.

The Mullahs must be punished, he shouted, and Mullahs were brought before him.

Dignified old men, said to have been implicated in the revolt in the south, were dragged through the streets in chains, there to receive the revilings of the monarch, and their sentence.

They were dragged forth again to the artillery parade ground, bound to the mouths of cannon, and blown to pieces.

Yet, within an hour of these executions, the King issued from the Arg citadel, having changed his mind yet once again. I was not there to see it, but there were plenty to tell me the news.

Amanullah proceeded to the public park, and called all men to him. He rated his hearers for their ingratitude and told them that ever since winning independence for his country his one aim had been to extol the name of Afghanistan in the ears of the world.

He complained with bitterness of the propaganda issued against him, and declared that he had never ill-treated the Mullahs, and had never given orders for the unveiling of women.

Not content with that, he ordered the printing presses to work, and had the walls of the city placarded with what all men knew to be untrue.

In the light of these events, what could the emissaries of the Shinwari rebels think of their King?

News came that evening of a further defeat of the Government forces at the hands of the rebels, and I decided to bring the war home a little nearer to Amanullah.

We proceeded that night to cut every telephone and telegraph line leading out of the capital. Amanullah had lost his best means of communication, and I knew how the suspense of the unknown would further fret at his frayed nerves.

Three times that night the King despatched mounted couriers to obtain news from the Shinwari front. Three times these men were sent back disarmed, and with uncomplimentary messages.

Meanwhile we maintained a ceaseless sniping, and a maximum of noise. We would allow the firing to fade away while we snatched a few hours' sleep, then horsemen would skurry under the very walls of the citadel, shouting and screaming and the sniping would break out anew.

The defenders spent a sorry time rushing from one end of the town to another to stave off first this attack; then that. Gradually, I was wearing down their morale.

Again that night I could have pressed home my attack, and I was sorely tempted to do so, notwithstanding the fact that the gates of the city were closed. Instead, well in the small hours, I decided to have another look at the panic-stricken capital, the more closely to view the results of my handiwork.

With the gates closed this might have presented some difficulty, but Bacha well knew how to open gates. On one of the gates of the city, well away from the main entrances, there was a small postern which was more than sufficient for my purpose. I had used it before, and I would use it again.

During one of the lulls in our sniping, five single shots were fired in quick succession. There was a short pause, and these were followed by five more.

In the crashing of the rain and the howling of the wind I watched that small postern, and after a wait of some twenty minutes I saw movement. A shaded light shone where there was before only abysmal blackness, and I moved forward, and was within the city.

A cautious voice greeted me as I stepped low through the postern. It belonged to Mahmud Sami,

a Turk who was originally imported into Afghanistan
by the Ameer Habibullah Khan as a military expert,
became a naturalised Afghan and the head of the
Military College whose students were now taking
such an active part in the defence of the capital.

"Art well muffled?"

Mahmud Sami put the question tersely, and
there was an element of apprehension in his voice
which, in the circumstances, was well understandable.
The fact that one of Kabul's principal defenders
should be consorting with the enemy leader might
easily have been misunderstood had I been
recognised.

However, Mahmud had no cause for alarm.
Further to protect me from the cold and the rain,
I had thrown a sheep-skin over my shoulders, and
this more than enveloped my ears. The end of my
turban I had in my mouth, so that little more than
my eyes were visible. Also, the long, loose sheep-
skin coat which I wore and the skin which I affected
round my shoulders made recognition of bodily
contours absolutely impossible.

"Caution, my friend. . . . Do not make for
the lights. . . . The Vazir, Mohamed Wali, is
abroad, and he has seen thee times enough."

I laughed, for Mahmud was most obviously in a
state of nerves. Clearly he had obeyed my summons
with the greatest reluctance, and he was chary of
being seen in my company.

He was unaware that I used him as a spy upon
the Vazir and that the Vazir was frequently unwittingly employed in checking up the statements
of Mahmud. When one deals with men who are so

open to bribery, it does not pay to take undue risks.

"Why don't you end this suspense, Bacha?"

I remained silent.

The man pleaded, for Kabul in its present state was none to his liking.

"Bacha—I can draw away our men and leave the way open for you to-night. The defenders are few. The soldiers are disgruntled. The King, he blows hot and cold, and knows not his own mind from one hour to the other. . . ."

I moved my shoulders. "All in good time, Mahmud," I countered. "All in good time."

"Tell me," he said at length, "why have you come?"

"To see Kabul in the grip of panic," I answered lightly, and left him. In truth, I was glad to escape his presence, for his very agitation invoked suspicion. His manner was so furtive that it called loudly for investigation.

Kabul, which should have been wrapt in slumber, was a city of feverish preparation. Frightened merchants were busily engaged in transporting their goods to places of safety, and in procuring wood with which to barricade their shops. On all sides were their moans and cries of despair, for the Kabul merchant does not lightly regard the coming of trouble and danger. In many ways he is a fatalist, but where his worldly goods are concerned he sees trouble from afar, and—rather than await its coming he goes forward to meet it with furrowed brow and lachrymose mien.

Even at that hour, the mosques were crowded with men who prayed that their ruler might be given guidance, and everywhere were gangs of men, working under the command of officers, busily engaged in unwinding barbed wire. Barricades were being erected in the principal thoroughfares, and round the palace itself miles and miles of barbed wire were being spun into entanglements. Kabul already bore the signs of a besieged city.

At a coffee shop where the proprietor, more intrepid than most, still remained open for business, I halted for refreshment. The freshly made green tea would be sustaining at such a time, and forsooth, I was weary with my long activity.

Several men were within the café as I entered, and amongst them I beheld one of my runners.

He was holding forth, and there was indignation in his tones.

"Would you countenance the killing of Holy men?" he demanded.

"Do you agree that they should be placed in front of the cannon and blown to pieces?"

"Is it right that their beards should be shorn, and that they should be heaped with indignities?"

"Nay," answered a man bolder than the rest, "but we dare not say so. Walls have ears in these times, and not for all are the mouths of cannon. A solitary revolver bullet is the lot of some, and others—they are even hanged."

"This Bacha Saquo," he went on, speaking softly, and with his eyes upon the scraggy hillman who had squatted in the shadows, "would he kill the Mullahs?"

My runner guffawed. "Kill the Mullahs?" he echoed. "By all accounts he would have killed anyone once, but since he has reached man's estate he has changed. He holds the Mullahs in veneration, and for him they are Holy. 'Tis said he met a Mullah when he was upon his travels, and that he can defy death. . . ."

"Do you think that he will take the city?" The speaker glanced round fearfully, as if afraid of his own voice.

"Do you think Amanullah Khan could stop him?" My man was sarcastic.

"But, Kabul will have none of him. He is but the son of a Saqua. . . . Imagine such a man with a court."

"A water-carrier's son," the others growled derisively.

I rose from the shadows, and made toward the hurricane lamp which gave illumination to the poor appointments of the café. I allowed the sheep-skin to droop from my shoulders, and the end of my turban to fall from my mouth.

"Merely a water-carrier's son," I echoed, my eyes burning with pent up passion.

I showed them my teeth, and grinned.

"Merely a water-carrier's son," I repeated, "but —one whose name is honoured in the hills as a warrior and a fighter. Merely a water-carrier's son who has defied the might of your King and who has laughed at the Royal soldiers who have been sent against him."

"Who is this stranger?" one asked querulously. "Methinks he is over bold and is in need of a lesson!"

"Bacha Saquo, the water-carrier's son," I replied ironically, reaching for my knife. "Perhaps you would care to try for the reward which is upon his life and carry his head to the palace?"

Astonishment and apprehension was upon these men, and they edged quietly toward the open street.

Once in the bazaar they turned and ran, crying: "Bacha . . . Bacha . . . he is upon us!"

Reaching for my sheep-skin, I followed them, crying in unison: "Bacha . . . Bacha . . .!"

The cry was taken up. The flying group became a crowd, and the crowd, a mob, all howling: "Bacha . . . Bacha . . . he is upon us."

Round the palace they swarmed—hundreds and hundreds of affrighted men and women, the latter quietly weeping, and the men calling upon the King to give them arms.

From the palace windows there came no sign. Amanullah Khan either failed to hear his people, or ignored them. It mattered not which. By a fortuitous chance I had excited them beyond measure. I had made the name of Bacha Saquo ring through the streets of the capital as it had never rung before.

The city was in the throes of great emotional stress. Before many hours there would be the reaction.

People would say: "We were assailed. The enemy was within us. We appealed to the King, and—he was silent. Is this the man who declared that he was the servant of the people the day after his father died?"

Always I remained on the outskirts of this milling multitude, for it is invariably there that one sees those who, in their turn, are there to see.

Ten paces ahead of me I discerned a form I knew.
I moved to the side, and caught a glimpse of a
saturnine countenance, and brightly gleaming eyes.

I edged up behind the figure, and whispered.

"Oh, brother," I said sardonically, "the people
are in a turmoil. They say that Bacha is upon
them."

Mohamed Wali, the Vazir, turned as in a flash,
and eyed me quizzically.

Twice he opened his lips to speak before the
words came, and then he spoke haltingly.

"Bacha," he gasped. "Have . . . have you
thy men within the city?"

I laughed behind my sheep-skin, for well I knew
what was in this man's mind. He, too, would have
Amanullah Khan desert his people. He, too, would
see that condition of mind where the people would
execrate the Royal name. Then he, who was already
such a power in the land, would know how to deal
with a simple son of a water-carrier, and Mohamed
Wali, who had so often knelt to the throne, would
ascend the dais and defy all to eject him.

So much had been in this man's thoughts since
first the people had reviled their King for his un-
Afghan ways.

But, this was not the moment to present this
man with a crown, and to invite him to throw me
to the jackals shrieking around us in their hundreds.

The light which was in Mohamed Wali's eyes
faded. He had sensed a great opportunity. For a
fleeting second he believed that he had only to raise
an authoritative cry. With that, Bacha Saquo
would have been admitted to an undignified yet

speedy death, and Mohamed Wali would have his heart's desire.

My unfeeling laugh shattered the roseate dreams which singed through his brain, and he regarded me none too pleasantly.

"More of your sport, Bacha!" he said, bitterly. "Mind that you tempt not Fate unduly."

I eyed him steadily.

"When do you attack, Bacha?" he asked on a different note.

"To-morrow," I answered, as if the matter was of no moment. "With the dawn, there will be an assault."

"You know that the King will resist? In the hours of light he will defend all. If you, Bacha, can enter Kabul without my knowledge, why do you not engineer a night assault?"

"I am my own commander-in-chief," I replied austerely, and left him.

CHAPTER XIII

AMANULLAH RESISTS

In the early hours, soon after dawn, I initiated an attack. I was true to my promise, but I had my tongue in my cheek, nevertheless. There are attacks which are pressed home, where the attackers hang on tenaciously in the face of all odds, and there are attacks which serve their purpose if the spirit displayed be such that the defenders are convinced that they must fight, or—die. My attack was of the latter order. This form of warfare can be costly to the attackers as well as the defenders, and we on our side sustained our full share of casualties, but before the day was over I considered the hours well spent. The King had seconded my efforts to the best of his ability, and had been an unwitting ally to my schemes. He thundered at me with his artillery, he filled his city with noise and smoke, he made war seem terribly near to the populace, and further harried the feelings of those pent up within the walls.

At sunrise, a large body of my men made a feint, and there was a heavy expenditure of ammunition which, however, did little material damage. Still attired in my sheep-skins, and riding a mettlesome horse, I made myself conspicuous—not with the idea of inciting my men to greater effort, for that was unnecessary, and not with the object of inviting enemy attention to my person, for that would have been rank foolishness, but—to allow the people of Kabul to see that Bacha Saquo, the brigand chieftain, was really menacing their walls, and to make positive that Amanullah Khan should be under no delusions as to the character of the force which was assailing his capital.

When this feint attack was well established, and all was obscured by the rush and turmoil of the engagement, I slipped away, and with my modern-armed men made for the fortified tower which is situate not far from the walls of Kabul, and is a dominating, defensive structure. The tower is really part of the Habibia College, and gives a command of a wide field of fire into Kabul itself.

From there we raked the city with a hot fire which eventually drew the attention of Amanullah's artillery. It was a mark which the gunners could not miss, and the position soon became untenable. I had, however, achieved my object in further lowering the morale of the defenders, and I evacuated the tower and joined the rest of my men in the village of Kalola Pushtah. Later in the day I fell back upon Bagh-i-Bala.

In the evening of the second day of my attack upon Kabul, I rested for some hours, but before midnight I was again in the city. I believed, wherever possible, that it was best to check up on my intelligence service with my own eyes.

Even in the space of a few hours the face of Kabul had changed for the worse.

The people had now come to learn of the reverses of the Royalist forces at Nimla, and they knew that the trade routes were blockaded and that the rebels of the south and the east were making headway. I had cut off all means of telegraphic and telephonic communication, and I planned on the morrow to cut off the water and the electricity supplies also.

As I wandered around this city which feared to go to bed, I heard the most exaggerated stories of the strength which I had at my command and, moreover, the voice of the people was beginning to change when the name of Bacha was mentioned. Intermingling with the crowds I heard less and less of this water-carrier's son. Rather I had become the Ghazi, the defender of the Faith, and the defender of the Holy Mullahs whom the King was still sending into eternity from the mouths of cannon.

Well muffled in my sheep-skins, I joined a group of Royal troops, lounging round a fire in the vicinity of the Arg. It was easy enough to fraternise with them.

Extending my hands toward the blaze, I remarked, surlily:

"The soldiers—always the soldiers—they can find fuel for fires. They can always depend upon food, and—their twenty rupees per month. . . ."

A gasp of indignation accompanied my words, and the sepoys viewed me angrily.

"Who are you?" one of them demanded, "that is so foolish to believe such tales."

"Twenty rupees!" He spat his disgust.

"You are not of Kabul, stranger, if you believe in such nonsense," he went on, aggrieved.

"Where," he demanded, waving his arms in a wide gesture, "are Amanullah's soldiers? Where is this great army which costs so much?"

"Aye, where?" growled another. "Nowhere, but in the pockets of the Vazir and our officers. A company which should be a hundred strong is but twenty, but the officers draw pay for the hundred."

"Ah!" said another. "And, our twenty rupees— it has mysteriously dwindled to four. Four rupees!" he exclaimed violently, "and three of those I have to send to my village each month."

He stood up in his tattered uniform and stamped the ground, reviling the name of the King whose presence he guarded.

I left the group, and wandered further, where there were knots of people assembled outside the Arg palace gates. All spoke with bated breath of the events in the capital that day following the shelling of the brigand chief.

The scenes that afternoon must have struck further fear into the heart of Amanullah. The merchants had refused to open their shops, and the people had been unable to buy food. The King, secure in the Arg, and not daring to appear in the streets, sent soldiers to open the shops by force. The merchants were dragged forth from their hiding places to trade, but none could command the prices which these men demanded. There had been riots, and a number of shops had been burned, and there were not sufficient troops to quell the disturbances.

Then, the people who had been forced to acquire European clothes approached the Hindu money-lenders, for they would have rupees for this despised raiment. But, the money-lenders would advance nothing on such security, and there had been more riots. The mounted police had been helpless, and one Hindu who had made a fortune in the disposal of Western clothes met his death by the same agency. A mob collected outside his house, flourishing unkempt bowlers, bedraggled trousers, and coats which had been cast off by the waiting menials of the West, and demanded money.

When none was forthcoming the mob piled the clothes in the roadway, sought kerosene, and set the whole on fire. Then they searched for the money-lender and found him, and threw him into the furnace.

The burning of the European clothes was regarded by the people as a gesture. It meant for them the throwing off of an intolerable yoke.

Near me were men discussing the matter, and the fines to which they had been subjected by the police for going abroad in Afghan clothes.

"Aye," muttered one, still writhing under the imposition, "I, for my sins live near the police station. The constable there is no friend of mine, and he would wait for me when I slipped through the bazaar to make some small purchase. Some days I would be fined, twice, or thrice, but once, I was caught no less than thirty times. Thirty times was I fined that day for appearing abroad without those un-Afghan abominations."

Could the King have heard what was being said within the shadows of his palace, he would have paused, and reflected on the situation. But his courtiers were still with him, assuring him that

the events in Kabul were but transitory, and that
he could afford to discount anything which a hill
brigand might do. As for the Shinwari rebels—had
not Royal forces been despatched against them?

I left Kabul for my headquarters at Bagh-i-Bala
three miles away—left it that it might contemplate
another dawn.

With the coming of light I continued to menace
the city, and there was some stiff fighting at times.
In Kabul itself, I was informed, all the public offices
remained closed, and the prices of foodstuffs shot
to an unheard of level. Then a runner brought news
of the gates of the Arg palace being barricaded.
Large stores of food and ammunition were being
carried within, and evidently Amanullah had determined that the time had come to make some sort
of a stand.

Also, as I could see, the King's aeroplanes were
busy. They flew off carrying messages of distress to
all parts of the country. Amanullah was calling up
the tribal levies. In one such call which was read
to me, he promised those who came to his aid
almost untold wealth, and an adequate supply of
arms and ammunition.

As the day wore on the first of these recruits
began to trickle into the city. I did not even pretend
to bar their progress. Rather did I send my men
out upon the roads to welcome them with cheery
cries and robust jest. The flow of humanity increased, and more and more did the streets of Kabul
become choked with the tribesmen. The King threw
open the magazines, and all who asked for rifles
and ammunition were supplied. Not to be outdone,

I disarmed several hundreds of my tribal warriors
and sent them into the city. Merely for the asking,
they were provided with ·303 rifles and ammunition.
Their ancient tribal weapons they were able to
stack on one side for emergencies.

As I knew would be the case, this great influx
into the city became a sore trial, for Kabul was
short of food even before its arrival. I resolved to
add to the confusion. I despatched Sayed Hussain,
one of my lieutenants, to Jubl-us-Siraj where is
situated the hydro-electric power house, and he cut
off the supply. Kabul was without light and electric
power.

I had by this time a number of mechanics in my
force. They did most excellent work. They accomplished mysterious things in the hangars on the
aerodrome, and more than one aeroplane caught
fire as the propellers commenced to swing. Also,
the King's armoured cars were made to do unaccountable things. Such mysteries were ever beyond my comprehension, but I know that my men
drew the petrol from the reserve tanks of these
vehicles, and substituted water. Thus it was that
so many armoured cars issued from the city never
to return.

The King's War Minister nearly went insane with
rage as these various matters were reported to him.
His was an unenviable task, for never did he dare
to tell the King of these catastrophes.

The majority of those whom the King had armed
cared not a pice for his cause, and once having
secured what they wanted, either returned to their
homes, roamed the city killing off rich merchants,

or helped to augment my forces. A large force of
Wazirs did, however, remain faithful to the King,
and these men, always ready for battle, fought with
spirit.

Bagh-i-Bala, where I had made my headquarters,
was near the aerodrome and within a stone's throw
of the British Legation, and for several days heavy
encounters took place in this neighbourhood. Had
the Wazirs been left to their own devices the order
of the day might have been different, but they were
required to fight under regular officers whose methods
of waging war had been learned in the office. These
ornate gentlemen would leave Kabul in their motor
cars just before ten o'clock in the morning. They
would take a dilatory interest in the fighting during
the day, issuing orders which none could comprehend
and none sought to obey, and than at four o'clock
they would call for their chauffeurs to return to
Kabul, there to cleanse their bodies of the grime of
battle.

One morning a group of such officers, who had
evidently read of the value of flank attacks from
some hastily perused text-book, crept under cover
of dead ground round to my right. They had with
them about three hundred men. I had few men to
spare at that moment, but—I had a lorry which
had been "requisitioned." Also had I the quick-
firing rifle which the Vazir had given me. I mounted
the lorry, and had it driven right in the midst of
these men, and I fired as quickly as I could renew
the magazines. It was a simple matter to pick off
the officers as we charged along, and the rest of the
men evidently found my quick-firing tactics none

to their liking. They took to their heels, leaving fourteen dead sepoys behind them and five officers.

That night I had the heads of the officers conveyed into Kabul. Next morning they were grinning at Amanullah's window from the walls of the Arg. I often wondered what were his reactions when he viewed this phenomenon.

On the fifth day of the fighting, I had my men strung out over a long line from Doukhtar to Kotal Kahir and I spent my time riding from one end of the line to the other, completely disregarding the rain of shells with which Amanullah favoured us. I knew that I was always a conspicuous figure from the walls, for it was part of my plan invariably to be in the forefront, but I think the shrapnel which caught me in the back was but a lucky accident for the gunner. True, shells had been exploding above me for some time, but I disdained them. The shrapnel caught me just below the shoulder blade, and I was rolled from my horse, in full view of the walls and all my men. The cut was a deep one, and I lost consciousness. When I recovered, there was a certain confusion. The Kabulis were lining the walls and shouting their derision. They were enthusiastic. In the ranks of my own men, however, I could discern no little alarm.

Throwing aside the hands which held me, I bade the hakim to hurry with his bandaging. Then, calling for my horse, I mounted again. I was unable to continue for more than half an hour before I had to dismount. All was going black before me, and it would have been foolishness to continue.

My injury gave the Kabulis a much-needed respite. It was during this lull that the British aeroplanes came from Peshawar and evacuated those within the British Legation. It was during this time also that Amanullah, heartened by the news of my mishap, issued forth from the Arg for the first time for several days. Again he harangued the people, yet again he had to display his extraordinary folly.

He took his place beside what is known as "The Pillar of Knowledge" which he had had erected shortly after he had come to the throne.

While the King declaimed, promising the people that the New Law would be withdrawn, and that all corrupt ministers would be dismissed, his hearers could see behind him this evidence of Amanullah's bad faith.

In the fighting which ensued after the death of his father, Amanullah had reason to declare an amnesty. Nevertheless, fifty-two leaders were arrested, court-martialled and shot, and to commemorate the event, "The Pillar of Knowledge" was erected. It bears the words: "In memory of the campaign which was in reality a battle between Knowledge and Ignorance."

Little wonder that the people openly accused him of breach of faith, and told him quite frankly that they refused to help him further.

That day Amanullah determined to have one more attempt at ousting me from my positions. I was then resting from my injury at Kafir Koh, and the King offered twenty thousand rupees for my head. The men of the bodyguard. and a large body of Wazir tribesmen issued forth, and fell upon us. Though one arm was still useless I could still fire my automatic rifle and I continued to fire until it burned hot in my hands. This encounter was one of the most sanguinary of the war, for we lost over two hundred men, and the Royalist casualties were heavier. Often the fighting was hand to hand, and when that day finished many sheep-skins were matted with blood, but—not Bacha's.

We broke off the encounter toward the afternoon, and the Royalist troops returned to the capital disgusted and disgruntled. Before evening, the men of the bodyguard, declaring that they had earned at least part of the reward, assembled outside the Arg demanding money. When this was not forthcoming, they too revolted.

Amanullah was nearing the end.

Before darkness fell that evening every available aeroplane was in flight. These were on their way to Kandahar. Others had already preceded them during the days that had gone before, and they carried the persons of the Queen and the other ladies of the household, and—all the crown jewels and the remaining gold in the Treasury. I was not to know that until later.

That night the runners came to me in a continuous stream.

The King sat with his brother, Sirdar Inayatullah Khan, in a darkened room in the Arg. He was afraid to have too great an illumination in case a shot would come crashing through the windows.

Finally, Amanullah signed a paper of abdication, handing over the throne to his brother Inayatullah

—he who should have been King in Amanullah's stead.

I, Bacha Saquo, had had my way. This King had been forced to ignominious flight. Actually, he left Kabul in his Rolls Royce before dawn.

But, what was it that that Mullah had said? He had mentioned many kings. More remained to be deposed before I could wear the diadem.

When news was brought to me of Amanullah's impending flight, I called for my horse and, with twenty troopers, I secreted myself in the shadows on the road to Kandahar. I wanted to be sure that this King was really running away, and not indulging in yet another subterfuge. Also, I knew how easily he could change his mind, and—I did not want him creeping back with the dawn, and asking for the return of his letters of abdication.

Oh, Amanullah was quite capable of doing this.

The snow had fallen deep on the Ghazni-Kabul road, and Amanullah found his way almost blocked. He had to proceed slowly, and I was able to keep up with his Rolls, riding easily away on his flank. Never did we lose sight of his headlights.

At Arghandi, some twelve miles from Kabul, his car became stuck in the snow, and for two hours I had unpleasant qualms while efforts were made to dig the vehicle out. Would Amanullah never go?

Those with the King eventually cleared a way. They tied rugs round the rear wheels, and these at length made purchase. The King's car slid forward.

To make certain that this leisurely departure should be a flight in fact, I called to my men. Hulloaing and shrieking, we made for the car. We could see Amanullah gesticulating wildly, beseeching his driver to go quickly. Suddenly, the car swerved. One of the rugs tied to the rear wheels had become jammed in the mudguard, and for a moment I thought the car would overturn in the snow.

I had hurriedly to alter my course, otherwise I would have been upon the King. Firing our rifles, and shouting shrilly, we circled, while a frightened chauffeur jumped from the car and cut free the rug. Then the car once more jumped to life, and with a swoop and a roar, we were after it.

We galloped headlong for over a mile, until indeed, the car was but a speck in the distance.

Such was the manner of Amanullah's departure from his capital.

CHAPTER XIV

KING IN NAME

WEARY from my pursuit of Amanullah, and exhausted, for my wound had not yet healed, I placed my command temporarily in the hands of my lieutenant, Syed Husain.

I felt that I could do so, for I did not take the obese Inayatullah too seriously.

When I was informed that he had appeared on the balcony of the Art while the Court Chamberlain read of his accession, I laughed, notwithstanding my fatigue.

"Go," I called to Syed Husain. "Go and prick the fat one. And, when you skewer his belly, there you will find three melons."

I had a letter written and despatched to this new King, in which I told him that he must either surrender, or prepare for battle.

Inayatullah did not immediately reply, and I signalled to Syed to proceed. The next morning he was within the city, and he had Inayatullah besieged in the Arg.

Shortly, the white flag was seen, and another King had come and gone. Inayatullah signed an agreement with me whereby he agreed to abdicate and to acknowledge me King.

The manner of his departure presented a problem, for Amanullah had gone with the last of the aeroplanes. Eventually Inayatullah winged his way to

Peshawar in a British aeroplane, and within a few minutes of his going I was in the Arg.

I was master of Kabul, and certainly master of my province of Kohistan. All seemed to be going well with me, but there were still many kings to be removed from my path.

However, I must dwell upon my triumph.

There was no little of pomp and circumstance attaching to my formal entry into the capital. Inayatullah's aeroplane had hardly left the ground before I entered via the principal gate, riding my charger. The bazaars were filled with my cheering soldiers, and the Kabulis, too, seemed glad to be rid of a family which could impose upon them such un-Afghan ways. There was, I admit, little of military precision in the comportment of my men. There were no blaring bands; the men did not march in rank, and they did not attempt to keep step; but—all bore themselves as victors and as fighters, even though they were unkempt and begrimed from a campaign which had been waged in the dead of winter and in gales, rain and deep snow.

My men did not require to march with mincing step in order to create an impression. All thronged the streets and windows to see the valiant men of the hills who had followed the water-carrier's son through so many vicissitudes until, to-day, he was King.

With a few of my companions I made haste to enter the Arg palace, and from there I sent out a formal notice intimating that I had assumed the sovereignty. From the people of Kabul I demanded written guarantees of allegiance—not because I

believed in their written word more than that which
was spoken, but because I wanted something to
brandish in their faces should occasion arise.

About fifty of my principal followers accompanied
me into the palace, and a most intriguing place we
found it. Of those with me only one had seen
European furniture before, and many of the appointments were quite beyond their comprehension.

They laughed loud and long at the long, white
baths, and refused to credit that mortals could go
to such trouble merely to cleanse their bodies when
there were streams ready to hand. These were the
first European baths that I, too, had seen, but this
I did not admit. Having dwelled in the land of the
Ferenghi I was credited with a knowledge of all
such things, and I was required to answer a host of
questions put to me by my brawny hillmen as we
made our tour of the immense rooms.

One of my men, Malik Mohsin, was a hoary old
scoundrel of seventy. I was to make him Governor
of Kabul, but when we first entered the capital he
had never ventured beyond the hills. He was an
immense man, well over six feet tall and broad in
proportion, and he was a large landowner in Kalakan,
the village of my birth. Because I had performed
a number of tasks for him when I was a boy the
old man was apt to give himself airs, and it was
frequently necessary to remind him of his place.
He could never entirely forget, however, that he had
had a King in his employ.

In one of the palace rooms there was a billiard
table such as I had seen in the bazaars of Peshawar,
and Malik Mohsin evinced considerable interest in

this piece of furniture. In truth, the old man had
been rather trying that evening, and when he asked
me to declare its purpose, I told him that it was a
bed specially imported from across the seas for
generals of renown and of giant frame. I assured
him that such was my satisfaction with his efforts
on my behalf that I would allocate to him this
unique bed. I bade him depress the side cushions,
to determine how soft the bed really was. The
dust cover I described as the bed covering, and I
assured the old man that now we were ensconced
in the Royal palace he would have to divest himself
of his clothing before retiring, this being the accepted
thing among the great men.

The weather was still desperately cold, and Malik
Mohsin's denunciation of all things foreign the next
morning did much to make me forget the hurt in
my back. He complained not only of the terrible
cold, but of the undue hardness. His principal
vexation was that he had been unable to tear away
a hole for his buttocks—an old hillman's trick when
lying in the open. For several days he carried his
aged bones with a limp, yet I doubt whether he
was any more uncomfortable than those of my
band who sought to sleep on down-covered mat-
tresses and between blankets lined with silk.

I did little more that night than to see that my
men were well fed. In the morning, after a night
spent on a thick-pile carpet—for I, too, distrusted
these Ferenghi beds—I assumed the mantle of Kingship, and began the construction of a Cabinet.

I had seen too much of Amanullah's court to have
any respect for too much learning or for courtly

manners, as such. Indeed, I distrusted those who
were learned of the arts. I could neither read nor
write, and I had found it no handicap. I could
hire for a few rupees those who had assimilated the
ways of the pen, and I determined that my Cabinet
should be one of action.

No bowing, lip-serving courtiers for Bacha.

My brother, Hamidullah, I made my personal
assistant.

Syed Husain, my principal lieutenant, who had
stood me in such good stead upon the field of battle,
I named as Minister for War.

As Court Chamberlain I had to have someone
who was acquainted with the ways of courts, yet
someone whom I could trust. Here I turned to Sher
Jan, lately Governor of my province of Kohistan.

As yet, there seemed to be little need for a
Minister for Foreign Affairs, yet I filled the position
with one Ata-ul-Haq. Abdul Ghafur I made Home
Minister, and the venerable Malik Mohsin, Governor
of Kabul, which greatly pleased the old man's sense
of dignity.

The Post of Minister of Finance was not an easy
one to fill, but at length I made Mirza Mujtba Khan
officiating Minister.

In the whole Ministry, only Sher Jan, the Court
Chamberlain, and the acting Minister of Finance
could read or write, which I considered to be just
what Afghanistan of my day required. With a
Ministry such as this there could be little room for
chicanery, and those meddling with accounts, which
proved the principal pastime of Amanullah's
courtiers, would be an impossibility.

My Cabinet formulated, I now realised, perhaps for the first time, that I had an army. Before I had a force, but during the progress of the revolution more and more had flocked to my banner, and yes —I had an army.

I realised only too well that if Amanullah had kept faith with his men and had paid them their salaries, he would have been in a position to put down disorder when the time for action came. I resolved there and then that no matter what happened, my men should always be the first to be paid. At all costs I must keep them securely on my side, for I knew not what yet had to be accomplished.

It was my Minister of Finance who gave me my first shock. I had bade him secure the keys of the Khazanah Ammirah (the Government Treasury) and these he apparently had no difficulty in appropriating. From his rather breathless account I gathered that they were still hanging in the doors of that normally well-guarded chamber when he repaired there to take possession.

His report was terse, and did not take long to deliver.

Briefly, it was that the Treasury was empty. I was aware that Amanullah had been extravagant, and that he had spent over a million pounds on his foreign aping, but never did I expect that I would walk into an empty granary.

I admit that I was both angry and chagrined when this dire news was brought to me, for the country had been ravished of three years' taxes in advance by Amanullah, and the speedy filling of the national coffers was going to prove a difficulty.

The assembled Cabinet heard the report of the Finance Minister, for this was a subject in which we were all interested, and many were the cries of consternation when Mirza Khan told us of Amanullah's shortcomings.

When, too, was added to this the report of the complete absence of the Crown jewels, I was beside myself with anger.

"Amanullah! . . . he is nothing more than a common thief," I stormed, and the Cabinet agreed, for the outlook was indeed dark.

I glanced round at the circle of blank faces, and found little inspiration.

I turned to Mirza Khan.

"As Finance Minister," I said, "what have you to suggest?"

My estimate of those who are learned of books dropped still further, for the man had nothing concrete to propound. At least, he had nothing immediately to his tongue which would provide money for the troops who were now hungrily awaiting some tangible token of the Royal regard.

I sent the man away with instructions to return in an hour with a prepared scheme for the raising of money.

He retired with ill-grace, and came back after an interval with many sheets of scrawled paper, and enough arguments to confound a regiment of scholars.

For a time I listened in patience, while he spoke of so many pies on this, and so many pirans on that, but at length I was constrained to interrupt.

It was then nearly noon, and I wanted money.

"How many rupees will all this bring in by five o'clock?" I demanded.

Mirza Khan eyed me aghast, as if he could not believe his ears.

"Five o'clock, Your Majesty?" Plainly he was troubled.

"Before, if possible," I rejoined. "If your schemes will not accomplish that, then you had better desist."

"Your Majesty," he stammered. "What can I say?"

I knew what he wanted to say. Had he dared he would have resigned his post, for I was none too pleased.

For answer I sent for the chief of police.

When this officer arrived, I interrogated him briefly.

"Do you continue in your post?" I asked him blandly enough.

He salaamed deeply. I had this man's measure. He was the type who would adhere to such a profitable appointment until he was prised loose with a sabre.

"Know you all the Hindu money-lenders of Kabul and others who have money?" I demanded.

The man hesitated before replying, for he could not tell what was in my mind. I did not desire to delve into his own private worries, however, and put him at his ease.

"Amanullah was so much a servant of his country," I explained, "that it is necessary for his successor to resort to the money-lenders. I require a loan from these men," I added with gravity, "but —it will be no part of your province to apprise them of the honour that awaits them."

He understood me perfectly. He was not the chief of police for nothing.

"You will take your men," I continued, "and as many of the bodyguard as you may consider requisite, and bring all money-lenders and others to the Arg immediately. At each man's house you will leave trusty men on guard—outside and not inside —in order to ensure that ill does not befall the owner's goods."

He salaamed, and went on his errand.

While this officer was performing his duties, I apprised Malik Mohsin, the new Governor of Kabul, of some of his. Although these surprised him, the old fox's eyes glittered as I spoke, and I knew that the Minister of Finance could shelve his worries for the time being. He need be nothing more than a cashier.

Presently, Sher Jan, my Court Chamberlain, who displayed an early flair for his duties, announced that the money-lenders and other moneyed-men were on their way, and that the first contingent had arrived within the palace. I walked to a window, and watched the procession as it was being shepherded through the gates of the Arg, and a motley one it was. There were no signs of privation here, and there was not a man who did not boast of a paunch which spoke of high living, and of a distaste for honest exercise.

Always had I hated these men, and their class for I had seen what their rapacity could accomplish. My father sought assistance of such a one when the time came for the marriage of my sister, and he paid until the time of his death. Indeed, the rapscallion who negotiated the loan went to considerable lengths to fasten the debt on to me, the eldest son, and would no doubt have succeeded had I not threatened to burn down his house, and otherwise displayed my resentment.

I was never the scholar to work out for myself exactly what my father was required to pay for this accommodation, but a student in Peshawar once amused himself with a long series of calculations. On the basis of one Pool in the rupee per month, he estimated that by then my father had already repaid the loan five times. He continued to pay sums regularly each month for more than three years more, and then the money-lender declared that I owed him an amount more than the original loan.

So it was all through the villages, not only of Afghanistan, but of Hind. The poor were all in the clutches of these men.

I admit, as these fat-bellied thieves wended their way to the Arg, my thoughts were of my own childhood rather than of the misery which these creatures had occasioned others.

I could not miss those protuberant stomachs, and my mind went back to many hungry days when there was no food for us because the money-lender had demanded his payment.

The garments which these men affected were clean, but poor in texture. When they were arraigned before me, these men would plead poverty —abject poverty, but—though they could lie with their lips there were waist bands which would take more than a little explaining.

I gave orders for a score of the more wealthy to be admitted, and I bade Sher Jan pay heed to the ceremonial of his office, and Malik Mohsin, the Governor, to be attentive to his duties.

For myself I seated myself upon the durbar dais for what was my first semi-public gathering, and I was determined that these men should realise from the outset that they were not dealing with a weakling like Amanullah Khan. I required money to pay my troops. They had it. My course was clear.

Under the marshalling of the chief of police, these twenty apprehensive men were drawn up in line before me. I had the Governor on my left, and Sher Jan on my right.

All salaamed, but I broke into their protestations of allegiance and their oft-repeated desires for my long life.

I did not trouble to prevaricate. I went straight to the point.

"Gentlemen," I said. "I regret to inform you that the State Treasury is empty and that the Crown is in need of money. I have called together the men of your fraternity, and out of those who have gathered here, I have done you the honour of selecting you. Briefly, the Crown requires a loan— a considerable loan. What would you suggest?"

Silence greeted my words, for none would take it upon himself to be the first to speak.

"Come," I chided banteringly. "You are not usually so loath to do business, and—here is a King who would enter his name upon your books."

With apprehensive glances they eyed each other. Then one spoke.

"Would the amount be much, Your Majesty?"

"Ten crores (£80,000) would be sufficient for the moment," I mentioned the first round sum of consequence which came into my head.

I heard the gasps which swirled along the line of frightened men, as my words sank home.

Now there was not *one* who spoke. All broke out into an excited gabbling like so many geese. All threw their eyes to heaven; all extended their hands towards me in supplication, and there was no one who did not plead his poverty.

I had my rifle in my hands. In truth, it never left me, and I extended the butt and caught the nearest a blow in the stomach.

"Cease this bleating," I roared. "Cease to bewail your poverty. . . ."

"But, Your Majesty," broke in one with more courage than the rest, "we are accustomed to lend the needy a mere handful of rupees—we are not bankers. Such a sum as you mention is beyond our means. . . ."

I allowed him to prattle, for I was enjoying the situation.

He took another bite at his courage when he saw that he was not interrupted, and I saw the crafty gleam which was stealing to his eye.

"Besides, Your Majesty," he went on, "there has been no mention of security."

He salaamed, and his manner was abject. It was as if he were less than the dust, but I knew what was coming.

"We are aware," he went on, "that Your Majesty is a great warrior who has beaten the armies of the late King. We are certain, such is your greatness, and such the intellect which radiates from your august person, that Your Majesty will rout the rebels who are in Herat and in the south and east, but"— and he licked his lips as he drew even more courage from his inner reserves—"that is hardly the guarantee to which we, as men of business, are accustomed."

Still I remained silent, and the rogue continued: "You are asking us, Your Majesty, to utilise our own convictions of your greatness as our guarantee for the return of our money. We have been told that the Treasury is empty. It is whispered that even the Crown jewels are missing, and—we are, of course, aware, that the taxes have been paid for long in advance. . . ."

I had resolved to be fair, and to allow these men to state their case. None should say that the King refused anyone a hearing. But, enough.

"Malik Mohsin!" I spoke peremptorily to the Governor.

"These men," I continued, "say that they have no money; then they say that the King has no security. As Governor of Kabul you should assist your King."

Malik Mohsin displayed some surprise at this manner of address, but he had the wiles of his years.

"Your Majesty," he said humbly enough, "these men lie. Without doubt they have the money, and Your Majesty can furnish security." He looked significantly at the rifle which was in my hands. His glance was not lost upon the assembled line.

Immediately was there a renewed outcry. Hands were wrung, garments were torn, and breasts were struck. The whole twenty of them were howling for their lives, and for those of their families.

I lifted my rifle, and pointed it to him who had been their spokesman, and I allowed my trigger finger a certain lively play. The man stood there waiting for death. Great globules of sweat appeared on his forehead, and he was patently a craven. Yet, even in the face of eternity he held fast to his money bags. Even in that tense moment, greed of wealth was greater than his regard for life. Glancing along that line of fear-worked faces, I knew that Malik Mohsin had been wrong, and that were my troops to receive their pay, subtler methods must be employed.

I looked in the direction of Sher Jan.

"My Court Chamberlain," I said with emphasis, "you will know where to conduct this man!"

Sher Jan did not, but he was equal to the occasion, and the wretch was marched out.

Rising from the dais, I held up my hand.

"This levee is adjourned for the time being," I announced. "These others will await outside until I return. I go to give this money-lender security."

CHAPTER XV

I FILL THE TREASURY

THERE were many apartments in the Arg palace well suited to my purpose. There were places beneath the ground level where much had happened in the past. With a new regime there was no need for any radical alteration. Only would there be a tightening up, and these apartments, which had been allowed to become dusty for want of proper attention, should again play their part in the country's administration. I was under no illusions. I had won Kabul by the sword. I had lived my life by the weight of my sword, and I must needs keep my kingdom by means absurdly similar.

But, in this problem of the immediate payment of my men, mere blood letting would not suffice. I had to produce something which would gnaw at the vitals of these pot-bellied money-lenders and Mohammad Zai Sardars, whose money bags I would slit.

And, I had promised security.

I would have killed this man, and those with him without the flutter of an eye-lid. I had shed my blood for these crows, and the world would be better if they had shed theirs. But—their tongues still had to wag. Moneyed men can hide their gold, and almost invariably do so.

I despatched an orderly for the court doctor, and I bade Malik Mohsin bring our man below where the walls were thick and none would hear his cries. Not that I minded over much who overheard these creatures' wailings, but I had a certain effect to produce upon the rest of his kin.

When dragged before me in this dungeon this man was practically inert with fright and terror, but I stuck my knife a little into his stomach, and the blood letting did him good. He crashed upright with a shriek, and once again let forth a torrent of verbiage, pleading for his life. According to his own account no poorer man existed in the whole of Kabul. Of course, he was reputed to be wealthy—what man of his trade wasn't? But, he had been unfortunate. Many men to whom he had loaned the greater part of his fortune had gone to the wars, and had been killed. Others had fallen foul of the tax-collectors, and had been rendered penniless. Others, because of the state of the country before I allowed my beneficent presence to appear, had merely run away. All was woe and desolation. The man nearly filled the compartment with his tears.

I held up my hand, and signalled to the hakim. "Bind up his right hand so that the blood will not flow," I ordered. "Bring pitch, and other of your wares, so that you may staunch a wound."

I gazed at this man of much money, and the sight was good. His eyes pictured a riot of conflicting emotion. He could still see his money scales, and on one side was his gold, and on the other his life. The balance swung, first this way and that, and meanwhile the man sweated. His fear produced in him a continuous tremor, and his teeth chattered in his excess of misery.

The preliminaries were brief. The man's wrist was bound, and the bandages curled up his forearm. I called for a heavy sword, and swung it. I turned to this cringer.

"You defied me in the audience chamber," I said, and I allowed my bulk to tower over him. "I asked you for money, and you said you had none. Then you spoke of security. You had changed your mind. Then, when you had my rifle at your breast, again you defied me. You were saying to yourself: 'If I am to die, this Bacha at least shall not have of my gold. There is my family. It shall not go poor.'

"But," I added heavily, "there are other ways."

Again I swung the sword.

"What will you give me for a right hand?" I demanded.

The creature shivered afresh.

"I place the value at fifty thousand rupees." I saw him wince.

"And, as for security——"

I nodded to the doctor, who pushed forward the man's arm. I swung my sword, could have sliced his right arm, but contented myself with only the thumb.

I picked up the member, and held it before this amazed man's face.

"Fifty thousand rupees before five o'clock," I said brusquely, "and—here is my security. Failing the money, your left hand shall follow your right thumb."

The fellow swayed and collapsed. I left him with the doctor.

Returning to the durbar room, I had all the money-lenders marshalled before me. I ascended the dais and addressed them.

"You are men," I stormed, "for whom my men have given their blood, and you display your patriotism by refusing me money. You asked for security. You shall have it."

I held up the blood red thumb that all might see.

"This," I said, "was formerly the property of one of you. It has now been ceded to the Crown. The Crown holds it as an emblem. It is security for the left hand of that man. It is also security for your right and left hands.

"The audience is terminated, gentlemen. The Chief of Police will inform each of you how much you will be required to bring. Those who fail to bring that which is apportioned, and seek to tender some lesser amount, will lose their hands. Those who are still contumacious, will lose of their feet, and noses also. And," I added darkly, "that need not exhaust the inventory."

These men could see that I meant what I said. I was no Amanullah Khan.

Before five o'clock I had the amount which I had specified. There were several amongst those who had been before me who appeared with less than the Chief of Police had considered them able to pay. They pleaded that they had been assessed at more than they possessed, and in proof of this, they pointed to the fact that their brothers in iniquity had made good the amounts for them.

Nevertheless, I considered that a King should maintain his word. True, I had my money, but these people required a lesson. Before the whole, and without troubling to escort them below, I slashed at their thumbs.

Sher Jan chided me afterwards on my precipitancy. He was the Court Chamberlain, and was somewhat aggrieved. He had the temerity to suggest that there were places set apart for the meting out of justice, and he eyed with implied criticism, the dark stains upon the audience chamber carpets.

I laughed. Of what moment were a few blood-stains to one who was accustomed to the hardships of the hillsides.

However, I saw Sher Jan's point.

I mention this incident in some detail for there are some who have not hesitated to aver that a summons to the Arg entailed farewells of one's family, and that there was no hope of returning alive. Many did return alive. It was only those who proved to be stupidly belligerent who felt of my anger.

These people never adequately realised that there are sacrifices which a people must make for the State. I had to go to extreme lengths in order to obtain a paltry sum with which to satisfy the men who had carried me to victory.

As may be imagined, with an extensive army, such an insignificant total did not suffice for long, and I had to resort to other means to procure money. The merchants, if they suffered, were in themselves to blame. They rocketed their prices, so that the money which I dispersed was soon dissipated. In any event, it returned to their pockets, so they could not grumble with any degree of sincerity if they were made to disgorge it again.

Yet, I did my utmost to economise. I had no use for the arts, and I saw no reason why State money should be squandered on the upkeep of such schools as Amanullah had started. I remembered how I had hated my hours with the village Mullah, and I was certain that all the school children would welcome the change of regime.

I closed the schools, and dismissed the teachers. The teachers grumbled, but had I retained them, I should have allowed them to give of their services under false pretences. They would never receive their salaries, for there was never more than enough to appease the army, and to meet my own simple wants.

Mirza Khan, as a Minister of Finance, was devoid of ideas. I had to depend solely upon my own initiative. I closed the libraries, the laboratories and the Royal Museum, and sold off the effects. Again the merchants displeased me, for the prices which they gave were absurd. They would give no more than a few rupees for a whole bundle of books. And, when I took action against them, they too pleaded for mercy!

The merchants! How perverse and obdurate were they.

Amanullah Khan had printed banknotes, and they had been pleased to accept them. Now, they said there was no money in the Treasury to back the notes, so they treated them with scorn. I could not fathom such ridiculous nonsense. What was money before, was money now. But I said I would print notes of my own. I set the printers to work, and the merchants flung the paper in the face of those who proffered it.

I had no metal from which to coin rupees, and as a temporary measure, and until silver should accrue, I issued coins of leather. They were properly marked, and bore the stamp of the Royal mint, yet these stubborn people would have none of them. The merchants were open enemies of the Crown, and means had to be devised to bring them to heel. If these means were somewhat unpleasant, then they had only themselves to blame. They cannot say that I did not try other methods before resorting to a certain amount of force.

For wealthy merchants who would not accept my notes I had to create an impression. Upon the aerodrome I had erected a series of tall poles. I bade the blacksmiths prepare iron rings, and prepare pulleys. I had sharpened stakes sunk into the ground at the foot of the poles. I gave orders that my officers were to regard merchants who defied me as guilty of treason. They were to have one hour in which to take leave of their families, and were then escorted to the aerodrome. There a further time was allowed them for prayer. No one can say that the King was not considerate. Then they were fastened to the rings which ran loosely with the pole, and hoisted up on the pulleys. At a signal, they were released, and retained to the pole by the iron rings, they would slide earthwards at speed and were impaled upon the stakes.

Malik Mohsin proved an adept at this work, and was apt to preen himself and to enlarge upon his dexterity. Certainly, it proved a most compelling means of raising money for the State, but the old man was prone to forget that the idea was mine. Also, he still prattled in an unseemly manner of the times when I performed tasks for his favour and his pice.

One day I rode to the aerodrome to watch Malik at his duties.

We walked up the line of groaning, retching men.

I gazed up at the poles and the pulleys, and ruminated.

"I have a new idea for aged braggarts," I said.

"We will hoist them up by their ears, and then let them slide. Old bodies impale just as well as younger ones."

Malik Mohsin took the hint.

There were those, especially men who had amassed large fortunes under Amanullah, and amongst these I number those who had been his principal recruiting officers, who sought to evade paying their just contributions to the State by escaping from Kabul and seeking sanctuary in the mountains. It was necessary to employ special posses of trusted men to hound down this type of ingrate. My men were very successful in seeking out these vermin. When caught, I had these gentry bastinadoed until they disclosed the whereabouts of their ill-gotten wealth. Then, that they might not further embarrass the State by their unseemly mode of living, they were either bayoneted or sabred.

For the poorer people who proved recalcitrant and would not accept the new regime I had to concoct other punishments. Wherever possible, I reverted to the ancient method of dealing with criminals, and after cutting off their hands, had them hoisted aloft on poles in iron cages.

Although several attempts were made upon my life as I moved about the capital, I continued to ride wherever I chose, and frequently without a bodyguard. Several times was I shot at, but more often than not I detected the movements of the would-be assassin, and my trusty automatic rifle spoke first.

Thereafter, there came a spate of attempts from the security of darkened windows. While this did not give me pause in my journeys abroad, and while it never occasioned me any disquiet, not even so much as a quickening of my pulse, I had to take cognisance of these efforts to do me harm.

It was a curious thing, this disregard of mine for what happened to my life. I was prepared at any time to defend myself with fury, but my reaction was always that of anger to think that there should be someone who imagined that he could best me at feats of arms. I was proud of my pre-eminence with a rifle or a revolver, and I would have none sully my good name.

As for my life itself, I can truthfully state that I valued it not. Always I had in mind the speech of the Mullah in the Khyber. He had said I would be King, and King I was of Kabul and of Kohistan and now I told my Cabinet and my principal lieutenants of this, Malik Mohsin had heard the story before, and this time he did not deride, and shake his aged sides with laughter. He knew it to be true. And, I told them of the second part of the Mullah's saying—that part where I should live as long as he, and for two moons beyond.

Each day, as I went my rounds, I would say: "Methinks I die to-day," and that gave them something on which to ponder. They were fully aware of what their position would be if aught should happen to their King.

Each night, before retiring, I would add: "'Tis curious . . . I did not die to-day!" And that gave them something for their thoughts in their sleeping moments.

It was as a result of this that I found myself surrounded by a body of picked men from my old brigand comrades of the passes. These men accompanied me everywhere, frequently to my annoyance. And, I knew why they held so fast. The members of my Cabinet, in consort with others, paid these men treble salaries to see that I came to no harm. Often I laughed in my beard when this cavalcade trooped behind me, and frequently I would put spurs to my horse and outdistance them, for none was mounted as I.

It was on these occasions that shots were sometimes rained upon me from balconies and windows.

It was Malik Mohsin who devised a way of his own to bring an end to these attentions.

He recruited a secret police, and when a shot came my way these men got busy. Whether they invariably secured the person responsible, I cannot say. Frankly, I was bored with such proceedings, and I took little interest.

However, many were they who were introduced to the underground apartments of the Arg, and one day, in an idle moment, I decided to investigate. Malik Mohsin was down there with the chief of police and his secret service hirelings.

They had a man in an iron chain who had already confessed to shooting at his King. I am inclined to believe that in this instance the confession was not merely something to mitigate torture, for as soon as he saw me, the man spat in my face.

I watched the subsequent proceedings with the more interest.

From a boiling urn suspended in the roof, small quantities of oil were poured upon this hound's naked flesh. Each time a fresh portion of his anatomy was selected.

Manacled, and kept at a distance by a file of soldiers, were the man's relatives and neighbours.

It took this man an hour to die, and then the spectators were released.

It was pretty work.

Of those who conspired against me in other ways, I had to mete out more summary punishment.

There was Sardar Hayatullah Khan and Abdul Majid Jan, two brothers of Amanullah Khan. One would have thought that men of that family would have had enough of intrigue, but no. Certain information was brought to me, and I was not one to take chances. It was suggested by one of my court that it would be more regular were I to convene a court-martial, and hear witnesses in order that regular depositions might be put on record. However, I was a King at war, and I could not afford to trifle with Fate and play with stupid conventions. I had them shot in the grounds of the Arg, and their bodies thrown into a nearby ditch. Another active with these erstwhile Royal brothers was Sardar Mohammad Usman Khan, the Principal of the Arabic College. In a manner I could understand his taking umbrage, for his institution had been closed, and its effects sold for what they would fetch. Nevertheless, I deemed it best to send him on the same journey. He, too, was shot, and deposited in the ditch.

In point of fact these men of learning, and of pseudo-learning, gave me considerable trouble. There were many students who affected to despise the rough ways of the King from the hills and were intemperate enough to voice their opinions. This much I was prepared to tolerate, but I discovered that it was a way of students to band together, and to discuss what they were pleased to define as "politics."

But these misguided colts had forgotten, or would not take the trouble to remember, that I had dwelt in Hindustan and had there seen the way of the students. Often while in Peshawar I marvelled that a Raj as reputedly powerful as that of the British should allow students to march in procession and openly avow their disloyalty. The most amazing things I heard in the bazaars of Peshawar—of what was to happen when the British were dislodged; of the rapine and looting that would go on in the cantonments, and—more often than not there was a secret service agent there taking notes, so that the British could not plead ignorance of what was transpiring beneath their noses.

I would have none of that, and when the secret police discovered a student conspiracy against my person, I took action. One Habibullah Khan was the prime mover, and another, Abdul Rasul Khan, his able seconder. They were arrested, and the Chief of Police telephoned to me at the Arg.

"What shall I do with these children?" he asked facetiously.

I was tired of these child-like gambols of the unfledged.

"Drag them through the bazaars by chains," I ordered. "Drag them by circuitous ways that all may see. Drag them over the stones to the aerodrome. Then, if they can still stand, shoot them. If they can't, impale them."

They were shot.

CHAPTER XVI

AMANULLAH CHANGES HIS MIND

In truth, I found this business of Kingship, very wearying. The continual strain of devising means of raising money was within my province, yet without it. I knew that as long as I could continue what were really my tactics of the caravan-raiding days, I could count on gold and the allegiance which it brought in its train. But—-whereas the caravans continually tapped new sources of supply and were in themselves an inspiration, the ground which I now had before me could not indefinitely continue to exude money under the rack. I knew that, and was frequently troubled.

For myself I longed for the carefree days when I roamed the hills and was master of all I surveyed. Here in Kabul, I was master, but I was not carefree. Every day brought its increasing burden, and burdens for which I had no taste.

I discovered that to sit in durbar and express opinions was far more enervating than the longest ride across the mountains. Sometimes I would throw up my hands in despair, for the situations which were propounded to me day by day followed me to my couch, and sleep and I were not even on nodding terms.

The sweet, untrammelled sleep of the mountains was that for which I craved, and sometimes, even when in the audience chamber, the desire for rest and quiet was strong upon me.

Sometimes I would dismiss the durbar, exclaiming:

"Let me be. I can think no more. I will rest."

Those about me had a wonderful propensity for arguing in circles. They would approach a problem, chew it over for an hour, travel an unconscionable distance in so doing, perhaps performing gyratory evolutions on the way, and then return to the point from whence they had started.

This may have been statecraft, but it was essentially irritating to one of my temperament, and excessively fatiguing.

Even the burly and brusque Malik Mohsin absorbed some of the atmosphere and became as bad as Sher Jan. And, Sher Jan was an adapt in mouthing portentious phrases which trickled over his tongue like the swift running waters of a stream. He could give to the most pointless phrases an emphasis that clothed them with an air of wisdom. He could speak for an hour on nothing at all if necessary, and when he had done, he would gaze round with the expression of one who had made a pulsating contribution to an absorbing discussion. As I have said, even Malik Mohsin caught of this tongue-twisting, and he, too, could talk to a prisoner for hours on end without the man in the least realising whether he was being awarded a grant from the State coffers or was being deprived of his life. Not, however, that the people paid much heed to Malik Mohsin's words. They were aware, as soon as they were summoned to his presence, that their hour had come.

Well I remember one afternoon when I demanded repose. The senseless chatter ceased, and I curled myself up on a settee, and covered myself with a rug. For once I fell asleep, and must have been there for an hour, when a hand on my shoulder brought me back to wakefulness.

"Habibullah . . . Sire . . . Your Majesty . . . !"

I glanced round the great chamber with its silken curtains, its elaborate glass chandeliers, some of them now chipped where I had relieved my feelings from time to time by firing my automatic rifle, the European furniture covered with costly damasks, and the great spread of soft-piled carpets, and for a moment I thought it to be a dream, so deeply had I delved after my much-wanted rest. The rug which I had thrown round me was warm, but rough. In point of fact I had snatched it from the floor, and its texture against the skin of my face made me think of the hillsides and of wayside caravanserais where I had often slept snug and cheered in the midst of my loot.

"Your Majesty . . . !"

I sat up with a groan, and rubbed my eyes. The court barber stood at a distance ready to offer his ministrations, but he caught the look in my eye and vanished.

It was Sher Jan who was shaking me, and I could see that he had news to impart.

"Your Majesty"—for once he went straight to the point—"Amanullah Khan has declared himself King again!"

I jumped to my feet, and cursed. With Sher Jan I was the reverse to kindly.

"You are the Court Chamberlain," I shouted, "and should know that when I sleep I am not to be disturbed for trifles. . . ."

"Trifles?" Sher Jan was shocked into surprise.

"Well," I exclaimed testily, "you would not call it a major calamity, would you?"

And, in truth, I was unable to take the news very seriously. That Amanullah Khan would change his mind and decide not to leave Afghanistan for the moment did not in itself surprise me. The man was capable of any mental twist, and he was a profound optimist. I knew that he was still in Kandahar, and daily I was expecting news of his final departure. Yet, his decision once more to proclaim himself King was typical.

News was not long in coming, for information of an unpleasant character seems to bear the wings of the bird.

There could, of course, not be two Kings in Afghanistan, and I had to take measures. This was much more to my liking, and I welcomed the diversion rather than deplored it. My men had been well paid, and they would be better for a little fighting.

The couriers who came to me filled in a story, the outlines of which I already knew.

When I chased the ex-King out of his snow drift, he continued on his way, and from all accounts had a most unpleasant journey. It was not until the third day that he succeeded in making Kandahar, and there the manner of his reception was almost as cold as the winds which he had encountered on his way.

It must have been a very strange entry for Amanullah Khan for he was well accustomed to the plaudits of the multitude. It was even said in Kabul by those who had accompanied him on his travels in Europe that he accepted the acclaim of the white Ferenghi of London as nothing more than his due.

He was the first Afghan monarch to visit that great capital, and it was said that he was foolish to do so, for he was entering the heart of an enemy country. Yet the people, so it was said, turned out in their fog, and applauded his coming, and—such was his regal air that he found it difficult to bow.

No crowds rushed out of Kandahar to greet him. Not even an official put on a ceremonial turban to do him honour, and when his travel-stained Rolls purred through the bazaars, the people showed very plainly that they had little sympathy for him.

This much I had been told, and it was mainly for this reason that I had largely dismissed the man from my mind, believing that he would not long be able to withstand this unfriendly air, and would depart.

There was a certain amount of drama attaching to the ex-King's arrival, nevertheless, but the drama was in Amanullah's own heart. What his feelings must have been in the circumstances, I could guess, and the anger which seethed within him must have been torture when he was forced to ask the Elders to meet him, they having failed to come to him.

And, coals of fire—he heaped them upon himself. In a long oration in which he spoke about the revolution and said some remarkably unseemly things about me, he had nevertheless to admit that he had made many blunders. He said, moreover, that he had been rash and misguided, and that in order to save bloodshed, he had abdicated in favour of his elder brother Inayatullah. But, even while he was telling his audience this, Inayatullah was boarding a British aeroplane for Peshawar, and I was marching into Kabul to take up my residence at the Arg.

Had he but known it, he was appealing to the wind, but with all solemnity, he asked the Elders to co-operate with him to suppress this dreadful brigand, Bacha Saquo, never dreaming that even then I was wandering through his palace with my men at my heels, sniffing at the atmosphere of courts.

The Elders of Kandahar did not receive his communication with any evident pleasure. They did not even go to the degree of meeting the ex-King with that fulsome flattery which can mean nothing. The majority of them retained a stony silence, but there were some bold enough to tell Amanullah to his face that though they admired his superb aplomb in turning to them in his extremity, but that it would be more fitting were he to crave the assistance of the fawning courtiers who had brought about his downfall. Others, even more downright, told Amanullah that Afghanistan could not entertain a family, the principal of which ran away from danger and that, therefore, they were unable to entertain his brother.

But, as I have said, the majority of the Elders maintained a dignified silence, and Amanullah decided that he would remain, and watch events.

Yet, even Amanullah should have been able to read the mind of the people. On the following Friday, the name of the King was omitted from the sermon.

To complete Amanullah's discomfiture, next day came news from Hind that Inayatullah had fled from the capital, and was actually out of the country. What was perhaps more to the point was the information that I had captured the Arg.

Within a few more days, Inayatullah had joined his brother at Kandahar, and the populace were presented with the spectacle of two deposed Kings parading their streets.

With the arrival of Inayatullah there seeped into Kandahar a number of the Royal guards I had refused to take into my employ, and these men spread stories of my methods in maintaining a steady flow into the Treasury. Yet, while the people affected to be horrified by these tales, they did not think to ask Amanullah to disgorge the gold he had appropriated, or to return to the country the Crown jewels which he was eventually to transport to foreign lands.

It was apparently the telling of these stories which caused the people of Kandahar to shake themselves from their lethargy, and to turn once again to Amanullah. They declared that if he forthwith rescinded all his hated New Laws, they would provide him with money and with men.

Amanullah agreed, and if that had been the end of the citation, the situation might have been a serious one for me, but I knew Amanullah.

Amanullah, in the face of the promise of the Kandaharis, proclaimed himself King for the second

time, and once having made the proclamation was
again the King who had stalked through Kabul, and
not the man who had abased himself before the
Elders.

He at once proceeded to form a Cabinet, and—he
chose the very self-same self-seeking courtiers who
had served him so ill in the past. A deputation of
Elders waited upon him to protest against this
procedure, but Amanullah was barely civil to them.
He declared that if he were not allowed to act as a
King he would depart for Herat, and raise his standard there.

When all this was recounted to me in the audience
chamber in the Arg, I glanced around at the long
faces which were around me, and smiled. As the
story continued, and we were told that the Kandaharis were slowly mobilising, and that detachments
of troops had already been despatched to Ghazni
on the road to Kabul, I looked at those pendulous
chins once again, and laughed.

Then, I am afraid I felt anger.

I leaped to my feet, and raved at the lugubrious
loons whose faces shone like fading moons.

"Your courage disappears," I roared, "because I
have sent so many of my troops to the eastward to
settle the Shinwaris. "What have I to fear from a
man like Amanullah—one who is composed entirely
of weaknesses, and who is hated by the people?"

It was Malik Mohsin who interposed.

"Your Majesty," he interposed quietly with this
new-won courtier's tone which he affected, "we
fear not Amanullah, and we fear not the fighting for
ourselves. We fear for you. Each morning you say

that you will die. If there is fighting near, you will be there, and—perhaps you will."

I saw what was in the old rascal's mind, but I was in no mind to allow this ancient misanthrope to have the last word.

"Fighting," I scoffed. "What fighting? Is not the road between here and Kandahar knee-deep in snow? Are there not places where it is completely blocked? It would take a month for troops to arrive from there. How can there be an attack?"

I crashed the butt of my rifle to the floor.

"Rubbish," I yelled. "Rubbish. We will send a few detachments to Ghazni, and that will suffice for Amanullah!"

But, when my anger had cooled, I realised that the snow would not lie on the roads for ever, and that there were tribes between me and this other King who, if they did not care over much for Amanullah, still looked upon me as an upstart and as little more than the son of a water-carrier.

So, secretly, I assigned Sher Jan, my Court Chamberlain, to new duties—duties which came easily and naturally to him, and which in the past had accorded him no little profit and amusement.

More than half of Amanullah's puppet Cabinet were in intrigue with Sher Jan, and I decided to send him forth among the tribes that he might waggle his oily tongue and dispense rupees which I would squeeze from the people of Kabul.

I told Malik Mohsik that he had to apply the screw more and more, and the blood ran in direct proportion to the rivulet of gold which came my way, Much of this money was placed in the hands of Sher Jan, and his instructions were to buy allegiance.

In the main he succeeded, but the warlike Verdaks, whose land was between me and Ghazni, would have none of him or me.

The early detachments which I sent in the direction of Ghazni were met by the Verdaks under Karim Khan, and his brother, Lala Abdullah Khan, and were routed. I had perforce to send larger forces, but even these failed to win a way through. These Verdaks actually captured two of my ammunition columns, and I was minded to move against them myself. I required action, and I was tired of the confines of Kabul.

My brother and I had several fights with these tribesmen, and I would have given much to have had them within my ranks. They were superb fighters, and would not accept quarter. When it came to battle, it meant that the fight went on until the last man was killed, and it was several weeks before I broke down the resistance of these men.

On two occasions I found myself surrounded by Verdaks when riding with quite a small escort. My magazine rifle was called upon to play the part of a company of men, and but for the fact that I think I could hit the side of a playing card with my eyes shut, I should have been butchered.

Yet, one day, when the second of these occasions arose, who should be in command of the Verdak party but Karim Khan, their leader. I did not know this until the fight was well advanced, and my rifle was hot in my hands, but the additional tenacity with which the tribesmen held on to their early initiative eventually made me realise that we were fighting no ordinary enemy.

Men fell around me with extraordinary rapidity, and I fired and fired again, until I believed that my rifle would burst under the strain. At length, when the press had thinned a little, I saw along my sights a turban with a gold embroidered edge. Something gave me pause, and that moment of indecision nearly cost me my life. A slug whirled by my ear, and there was a man before me on horseback, young, and handsome, and extraordinarily virile. He had in his hands an ivory-butted jezail, the contents of which had so nearly accounted for me, and he now held it by the barrel. He lifted it high, to crash down the stock upon my head, but he knew not of what my horse was capable. Obeying the sudden pressure of my knees, for seldom did I need to touch my reins, his pretty hoofs stamped, and he was a yard away. The stock came thrashing through the air, and the impetus was such that the wielder was nearly unhorsed.

I covered this man with my rifle.

"Your name?" I demanded.

A grim smile passed over his face as he replied: "Karim!"

I might have known.

"I will not slay thee," I said, panting with the exertion of battle. "Call off your men, and I will accord you much honour."

But this man, looking down the muzzle of my rifle, merely laughed. And, he laughed loud, and my wrath was great.

He knew what was in my mind. He could discern the subtlety behind my glib invitation.

"Fool," I burst out. "More than the Verdaks have tried to deny me my destiny, and they have all died. Yet, with thee I would stay my hand."

He raised his head proudly.

"I do not crave for favours of a water-carrier's son," he retorted grandly.

"So, you would despise me?" I slipped from my horse.

"Would'st care to cross steel with a water-carrier's son?"

For answer he, too, dismounted.

Sensing the altercation which was proceeding between the leaders, both sides had gradually broken off the engagement and there were two ranks of men to observe the preliminaries.

There was dead silence as our swords clanged. Not a man spoke a word throughout that long duel, and all that I heard were grunts of approval and of dismay or of approbation as one or other of us secured a temporary advantage.

Karim Khan was a fine swordsman, and he was as agile as a cat. Moreover, he had thin Persian riding boots of soft, scarlet leather, whereas I had heavy boots after the Russian cavalry fashion. These impeded my movements in the snow-sodden ground, and I had to exert all my wiles.

Karim Khan was no orthodox fighter. He depended largely upon his ability to twist his torso and on the suppleness of his wrist, and against such tactics I had to forgo all I had learned upon the parade ground, and to revert to the days when I was a brigand, unlearned in the parry and thrust measures of the military. It was speedily borne upon me that this was no time for the theatrical if I were to retain my life.

While I was thinking thus, this man's blade was playing like lightning, and I could hear the appreciative "Ahs!" of his men. Twice he pricked me in the region of the heart, but my heavy sheepskin coat saved me—that and a backward twist—an old trick well-known by the boys of Kohistan.

At long last I slashed him on his right forearm, and his movements lost some of their speed. But, changing with amazing dexterity to his left hand, I found him still a formidable antagonist. Again, I admit with a certain stroke of fortune. I caught him, and upon the neck, and the blood gushed down his shirt. I started back, prepared to drop my blade, for I would preserve this young man; still I thought longingly of the access of strength which would be mine if the Verdaks would accept me.

That was almost a fatal mistake. In that moment, I allowed my eye to fall from his, and in the same instant he hurled himself upon me. A quick side step, and I had recovered, and I had my sword through his vitals.

He fell backwards, a strange smile upon his face. I twisted my right wrist, and my sword came red from him. He crashed heavily to the ground, and I made toward him, for he I could see that he was spent, and had little strength.

His eyes gazed into mine as I stepped forward, and there was a momentary galvanising. This man still had life. Before I could guess his intention, his hand groped at his girdle, and a knife came hurtling toward me.

I ducked, for the knife came point first.

Karim Khan lay there gasping.

"Is that the way to treat a soldier and a conqueror?" I demanded angrily.

"'Twas the assassin's knife for the assassin," he muttered, almost with his last breath. 'Twas a knife to kill my brother's murderer . . . a knife to rid Afghanistan of the fiend that thou art."

He stopped, his eyes glazed and he was dead.

The incident made me angry.

"Never again," I shouted, "will I show kindness to another man. I offered this man his life, and he laughed at me. I fought him fairly, and I would ease his passing moments. He threw a knife at me, and called me assassin. Enough!"

However, the death of Karim Khan broke the resistance of the Verdaks. They always remained my implacable enemies, but they had no heart to stand between me and Ghazni in force.

I was enabled to occupy the place before the forces despatched by Amanullah could plough their ways through the snows and arrive on the scene.

CHAPTER XVII

AMANULLAH'S LAST STAND

WHEN I declared that I had no need to be afraid
of Amanullah, I did not boast. When I spoke of the
difficulties of the road which lay before him, it was
but the truth. But, I then had in mind the vanities
and the innate weaknesses of this would-be monarch
who liked not personal combat, and the character
of the terrain through which he had to march.

Much, however, depended upon the attitude of
the clans. If they elected to believe Amanullah
when he said that he rescinded all his reforms, they
might elect to fight for him against me. On the other
hand, though they still might not be for me, their
hatred of a man who had done so much to antagonise
them in ways which no true Afghan could stomach,
might cause them to bar his way to Ghazni.

There could be no gainsaying the fact, however,
that the Kandaharis were keeping to their word,
and were massing to the banner of Amanullah and,
when on March 26, 1929, word was brought to me
that he had at length marched from Kandahar,
the army with him was large and well equipped,
Not only had a large proportion of the tribes of the
south thrown in their lot with their old King, but
a formidable body of Hazara fighting men had
helped to swell his legions.

Yet, I could not entirely eradicate from my mind
the thought that these men would be lukewarm.

and that when the time came for them to endure
the privations of the march and the hardships of
campaigning; when they saw their own brothers
cut down by the sword and when their womenfolk
complained because the men were at war and the
fields remained untilled, these men would ask themselves: After all, who is this King? Can we really
trust him? He has made promises before, and has
broken them.

Such thoughts are demoralising. They seep
through the morale of a force such as had gathered
to the aid of Amanullah, for—a civilian army thinks.
It is not like a regular army which has been drilled
and drilled until it acts and obeys by instinct.

The circumstances being as they were, I saw no
need to despatch over large forces on the road to
Ghazni, though some of my followers would have
me act otherwise. They believed that all was at
stake on this particular issue, but I laughed in their
faces.

And I could afford to laugh, for Amanullah, when
he marched out of Kandahar, covered no more
than three miles before he called a halt. He encamped at Manzil Bagh, and there spent four days
reviewing his men.

Why did he do this? Why did he not press on
the road to Ghazni, and the capital? I believed
that I knew why. He would have his advance guard
under Abdul Ahad Khan well ahead before he
sniffed of the dangers of campaigning.

Even here Amanullah had to display his vacil-
latory weaknesses, for had he pressed on after his
advance guard, and deployed his considerable army

as a general would, he could have taken Ghazni, for the place was no easy one to defend.

As it was, he allowed Abdul Ahad Khan, a man of no outstanding military attainments, to forge ahead. All the way this force met with considerable opposition from the tribes, and when it reached the gates of Ghazni it faced a heavy, hostile fire.

My forces there were little more than detachments, for it was no part of my campaign to hold Ghazni at all costs. I was ready to fight, but I was determined that when the battle was fought it should be on terrain which I had selected. I could see the weaknesses of Ghazni, and I never allowed sentimental considerations to weigh with me when I was considering my plans.

Had Abdul Ahad Khan pressed home his attack, he could have had the town for the asking, but he knew not how to hold his men, and his strategical knowledge was a minus quantity.

In the meantime, Amanullah was making his leisurely way toward the north. It took him sixteen days to cover the distance, and everywhere along his route he was subjected to sniping from the local tribesmen. The tribesmen did not regard him with favour, but they might have remained quiescent if he had maintained discipline among his host. He had thirty thousand men in his train, moving not as an army, but as a marauding gang of pillagers. The rate of progress was such that there remained plenty of time for unlicensed expeditions by the way. Dozens of villages were sacked and looted by Amanullah's men, and as he advanced he left behind him a countryside only awaiting an opportunity to exact vengeance. Many of the tribesmen did not wait. Especially at night, the army was subjected to a grilling fire, and always on its heels were those ready to snatch at stragglers. The only cohesion which this heterogeneous force displayed was a marked disposition not to be of the rear-guard. Those who lagged here were certain of short shrift from the tribesmen, and the deaths which were meted out were not the clean, easy ones of battle.

It was frequently suggested to me in Kabul that I should march out and give Amanullah combat, but that was the last thing I desired to do. I had able officers barring his progress, and I believed that this man would defeat himself without any aid from me. I was ready at all times to proceed to Ghazni, but if a major battle could be avoided, the advantage would be mine. I would still that Amanullah would depart the country bereft of the satisfaction of military honours.

Amanullah was badly served. In the fighting which went on around Ghazni his preponderance in men gave him many a strategical leverage, but he was no opportunist. Once having taken a village or a hill it was never difficult for his courtiers to persuade him that the military situation demanded evacuation. A considerable amount of money changed hands to secure this satisfactory state of affairs, and I kept Sher Jan well supplied. Amanullah never even guessed of the truth.

Here Amanullah spent two weeks in fruitless endeavour, his tribal levies, improperly led, proving more of a hindrance than a help. Amanullah did not entirely trust the tribesmen and he was even suspicious of the Verdaks who had gone to quite extraordinary lengths to display their antipathy toward me. Considerable bodies of these men were ready and prepared to render him every assistance which they could accord, but Amanullah, in his wisdom, held that these people who had waged a bitter war with me were secretly in my pay, and were only offering their assistance in order that they might sieze his person and convey him prisoner to Kabul.

So much did Amanullah's obsession respecting the loyalty of the tribesmen play on his mind that he eventually decided to disband his tribal forces and to rely entirely upon his regular troops. And, the tribesmen, despatched to their homes, broke out into revolt in his rear. Amanullah's communications with Kandahar itself were menaced, and he was in a quandary.

There were those in his inner circle who advised him to break off the battle for Ghazni and to chance all on one desperate thrust at Kabul, but Amanullah would not face the perils which beset him on the road to the capital. And, on May 14, he gave orders for an immediate retreat upon Kandahar.

In vain were efforts made to dissuade Amanullah from this course, but he remained adamant, and actually left for Kandahar ahead of his men, leaving his army to fend for itself.

As soon as news of Amanullah's departure was brought to me, I ordered all available forces to harass his rear.

The ex-King's army was thoroughly demoralised, and spread itself over the countryside without the least semblance of discipline, and my advanced forces had no difficulty in cutting a way through them and in speeding Amanullah's departure.

On several occasions, by riding hard through the hills, my men got in advance of Amanullah and his escort, and there were a number of sanguinary encounters wherein not a few of this man's personal bodyguard bit the dust.

Amanullah's progress became a rout, and it was with extreme difficulty that he reached Mohmand, the last post on the Kandahar road. More than once he might have been killed or wounded, and he was thoroughly spent when he reached this encampment.

He did not attempt to enter Kandahar, but sat down exhausted at Mohmand, and issued his second writ of abdication. He declared that he would strike for Chaman in British territory, in the hope of evading the pursuing forces of Bacha. Such was his plight that he could not even wait the arrival of his wife and other relations from nearby Kandahar, and he issued instructions that they were to join him on the way.

At dead of night, Amanullah crossed the border in his car, and was safe in British territory. His ten years' reign was definitely at an end, and I was in the saddle.

A few days later he was in Bombay preparing to sail for Europe. With him were his brother, Inaya-tullah, and most of his relations.

It had been a clean sweep, and I had had my way.

The name of Amanullah was execrated, not only because of his obnoxious reforms, but because he had failed in military endeavour when a determined fight might have won him the day.

In no circumstances would Afghanistan pay heed
to any of his nominees for the throne, and the way
was clear for Habibullah Ghazi, the Beloved of
Allah; the Knight of the Faith.

Had I not disposed of a monarch who had done
everything to belittle and malign the Mullahs and
his Faith? Was not I justified, therefore, in assuming
these titles?

But, the Khyber Mullah! Indeed was he a man of
remarkable prescience. Though the way had been
strewn with departing Kings there was still another
who would dispute the throne with me. In dealing
with him I had not the same influences which
restrained me in my actions with Amanullah. I
could afford to be ruthless. He was a soldier, and he
well understood what were the fruits of defeat.
Also, his death would mean nothing to the country.

This upstart was Wali Ali Ahmad Jan, a general,
whom Amanullah had despatched to quieten the
eastern tribes. He was remarkably successful
amongst the Shinwaris, whose confidence he secured,
and his popularity tended to distort his judgment.
He was a cousin and brother-in-law of Amanullah,
and as is often the case with families, he conceived
the most violent dislike of the ex-King. Indeed,
so frequently did the man give vent to his feelings
in this respect and so often did he tell Amanullah
what a mean thing he was, that he was degraded
and disgraced on half a score of occasions.

These two men would engage in wordy warfare
even in the audience chamber, and the court was
often scandalised by the bickering which ensued
between them.

In these heated altercations the general would not hesitate to remind Amanullah of peccadilloes which were family secrets, and which were better left unmentioned; and in return Amanullah would scoff at Ali Jan, and insult him, so that the general would bristle with anger. These unseemly wrangles only ended when Ali Jan became incoherent and speechless with anger, for Amanullah was an adept at the gibe, and knew exactly how to get under that rascal's skin.

There was one such incident, which followed one of these angry brawls, where Ali Jan so far forgot himself as to allow his hand to fall upon the hilt of his sword. In an instant Amanullah was on his feet, calling for his guard, and he had his brother-in-law under arrest. He swore that this impertinent man should die, but Amanullah's mother, who was also Ali Jan's aunt, interceded, and the general was spared.

This man had been sent to the eastern provinces to get him away from the court where his presence was obnoxious to Amanullah, and when he heard that his brother-in-law had abdicated, he had the temerity to declare himself King. He issued a proclamation to this effect at Jalalabad, and he took the opportunity of saying things about me which I was able later to throw in his teeth.

He called me an ignoramus, and an absurd upstart, and he promised all who would support him large rewards and high estate. Those who stood in his way or sought to argue with him he punished severely. By this means he rallied a not inconsiderable following.

He announced his intention of marching on Kabul where, he said, he would give himself the pleasure of cutting the water-carrier's son into little pieces, but procrastination was too firmly a part of the Amanullah family for the ex-King to have the monopoly.

Ali Jan spent days in haranguing and reviewing his men, and in the meantime I sent Mahmud Sami against him, and Mahmud was experienced in war as was the general.

Also, quite a large part of Ali Jan's soldiery had been recruited from Kohistan, and the men of the hills had always a regard for my person. When, therefore, these men heard of my successes and were informed by Ali Jan that they would be required to fight me for possession of Kabul, they deserted him, and threw in their lot with me.

This was a great blow to the pride of the self-styled King of Jalalabad, and news of his storming and raving was brought to me. Some said that Ali Jan worked himself into such a rage that he eventually fell to the ground in a swoon.

However, he survived the shock, and leaving Jalalabad in the hands of one he was pleased to term "Regent," he marched to Jagdilak. But, instead of proceeding to war, he spent days compelling even individuals he met on the wayside to accept him as King.

I realised, however, that I had in this man a most formidable rival. I had scoffed at the efforts of Amanullah to retain his throne, but Ali Jan, notwithstanding his age and his eccentricities, was an experienced general when he got under fire, and moreover, notwithstanding the desertions which had taken place, he still retained a considerable army, and he was well supplied with arms and ammunition. He had a plentiful supply of machine-guns, and even some artillery.

Consequently, I did not dally with this man as I did with Amanullah, and I despatched a large force to intercept him. We eventually camped at the Caves of Mullah Omar, only six miles from Ali Jan's most forward outpost.

From there I sent a deputation under the white flag, demanding this so-called King's submission, but instead of replying, he made my deputation prisoner.

He resolved to fight me, but he made a most serious blunder in the disposal of his forces. The desertions from his ranks should have warned him that the men from the northern provinces were for Bacha rather than for Ali Jan, yet—he placed men from these districts in the van.

When the two forces met, these men from the north refused to fire, and we, too, held our hands. There was a momentary impasse, and then these men also came over to my side, bringing with them all their arms and considerable quantities of ammunition.

More trouble was to accrue for Ali Jan, though he was able to extricate himself from a fight that day. He dispersed large sums of money in an effort to win the allegiance of further clans of the Shinwaris and Khogians, forgetting the blood feuds which exist between these tribes. One of the principal tribal leaders, Mohammad Shah, came secretly to me, and informed me of all Ali Jan's promises and plans.

I loaded this man with money and promised him great advancement if he succeeded in disrupting Ali Jan's forces.

When he returned, the general had been apprised of his going, and again Ali Jan nearly died in his fury. A fight ensued, in which Mohammad Shah was victorious. He looted Ali Jan's arsenal and routed his followers after a bloody conflict, and the old man had to fly for his life with his two sons. He had a very narrow escape, as there were many there anxious to secure the reward which I had offered for his apprehension.

Ali Jan succeeded in making his way to the Laghman Valley where he was taken prisoner. He was actually on the point of being sent to me at Kabul, when tribesmen friendly to him appeared on the scene and effected his release. From there he made for the Kunar Valley where he suffered untold hardships, but managed to slip through to Mohmand territory and thence to Peshawar.

As soon as Amanullah proclaimed himself King for the second time, he made for Kandahar, and made his submission to his brother-in-law, and he was still in Kandahar when I finally routed Amanullah. Then, the stupid man had sufficient optimism again to declare himself king.

It did not take me long to deal with him, for I now had him bottled up in a city from which it was difficult to escape.

When my men appeared at the walls of Kandahar, the terrified people opened the gates, and Ali Jan, with a few of his followers, sought to fight their way out. There was a terriffic fight, and everyone of the men with Ali Jan was cut down before the old fire-brand was taken, but taken he was.

He was brought prisoner to Kabul, and I allowed him to cool his heels in a dungeon in the Arg for a few days. Then I had him dragged out and produced before me in the audience chamber.

Even there the man defied and reviled me, but I told him that his time had come.

I reminded him of all the unseemly epithets which he had hurled at me, and the insulting language he had used in his references to me.

I had the old scoundrel bound, and placed upon a donkey. He faced the animal's tail, and in this ignominious fashion he was paraded through the streets of Kabul. After this exhibition he was taken to the aerodrome and tied to the mouth of a cannon. He did not remain there long.

CHAPTER XVIII

IN THE SADDLE

Now, indeed was I King, and with military cares cast aside for the time being, I had moments which I could devote to the task of consolidating my hold. Solidly behind me I had the men of the north. Those to the south had perforce to accept me by force of arms, and those to the east had been largely won over by the soft cadences of Sher Jan.

Yet gazing around the Arg palace I knew that something had to be done were I to receive and retain the goodwill of the nobles and upper classes. My warriors were of the hills, and despised the effeminate trappings which went with the Arg, and knowing their feelings in the matter, I found it difficult to chide them. To be truthful, it was not in my heart to do so, for I was really at one with these simple ruffians.

My sojourn in the land of Hind, however, told me that it was perhaps incongruous for my retainers to wash their muddy boots in the porcelain hand basins, and to hang their bandoliers from the candelabra. I did not criticize their actions when they removed the expensive rugs from the floors to keep warm their pack animals at night, for the weather was still cold. I decided, nevertheless, that a certain decorum might be invested in my court were I to espouse a lady more accustomed to the ways of kings than was I.

My present wife, a lady of the hills, was an excellent woman, but in no sense could she be called a queen. Her gnarled hands, and her swelling frame were exteriors which went ill with court life. She remained exactly what she was—a hardworking, painstaking consort for a man who dwelt in the mud huts of the hills. She was unhappy were she not working. Her principal relaxation was to knead the dough for hill bread and to gossip with the other women while so doing. Domestic labours such as this hardly went with a diadem.

Time and time again I remonstrated with her as she squatted in the palace grounds plastering her cakes on the oven.

"Woman," I exclaimed with hauteur on the occasion I have in mind, "desist. Give of this work to the menials, and retire to the palace and your handmaidens."

Still kneading, she glanced up at me.

"Why should I be cooped up like a hen?" she retorted. "Am I not a free woman of the hills?"

"You are the wife of the King." Sometimes she could be extraordinarily dense, and she roused my anger.

And, the foolish creature clucked, like the hen she despised.

"Wife of the King!" Her laugh was unseemly, and still she thrust her hands into the dough.

"You forget. You are the consort of Habibullah Ghazi."

She rose from her sitting posture, and faced me, clad as she was in the rough garments of the hills.

"I am the wife of Bacha Saquo," she returned quietly. "As for the King, if he would have a wife who would play the part of queen, let him take one!"

Another abdication.

I took the hint, and married a woman of high lineage—a relative of the departed Amanullah. My purpose was not only to garnish my court, but to win over, thereby, those who were still sympathetic towards the cause of the ex-monarch. Also, such a marriage raised my dignity, and placed me on a plane where I could contend with those high born who found it difficult to restrain their sneers, when they mentioned the name of their King.

I would not describe this as an ideal union, for the lady remained aloof, and sought vigorously to inculcate in me the ways of the courtier. Especially did she speak with scorn of the cock fights which I staged in the audience chamber. Such spectacles, she said with an arch primness, were for the boors of the bazaar, and not for the King. But here, at least, I would accept none of her chiding, for these cock fights were the breath of my life.

Every Friday, after the Faithful had attended their prayers, I had criers make their way through the bazaars, crying to the people to bring their cocks to wage war with the King. Only those with the most mettlesome birds knew that they might compete, for I had some of the bravest fighters ever reared in Kohistan. Any man in my home province who possessed a bird of outstanding merit knew that he could expect rich reward from his King merely by transporting it to Kabul.

These weekly contests became quite a feature of life at the Arg. A circle eighteen feet in diameter would be drawn upon the carpets of the audience chamber, and a peg driven through the centre.

We retained the ancient manner of betting for these bouts—a time-honoured custom which had been evolved to flaunt the old-established laws which forbade the placing of large sums on the results of these encounters.

More often than not a man would approach the court bookmaker and proffer an old whip to the value of a few pice. There would be a whispered conversation, and lo, the whip would be entered as a camel, or a square of land.

The cocks, which I had specially reared, were never less than eighteen inches in height, and I fed them on cream and wheat. I never allowed them to be armed with metal spikes, for these were apt to bring a contest to too sudden an end. When our cocks fought, they fought.

The excitement on these Friday afternoons did much to banish the cares of state, more especially as a bout seldom went by without a contest of a more sanguinary nature being fought on the outside of the ring.

Feelings invariably ran high on these occasions, especially when men staked their all, and lost, and when knives were drawn my soldiers would intervene.

At the conclusion of the cock fighting, those who had taken umbrage would themselves be introduced to the eighteen foot circle, and each would be provided with a dagger. There they were allowed to fight to their hearts' content, and there would be

more wild betting on the results. I had men specially
deputed on these occasions to remove the bodies,
and to sand the arena for each succeeding contest.

It was in an atmosphere such as this that the
thought came to me that Afghanistan should cele-
brate its day of independence from the dominance
of Amanullah. I issued orders that this should be
done, and I promised the people high revelry.

On the morning of the day I had nominated, I
betook myself to one of the high windows of the
Arg—a favourite scouting place of mine—and surveyed the scene through my binoculars.

And, I laughed, for this was the land upon which
Amanullah would impose the mind of the West.
There were the men he would see entrammelled in
European trousers.

Near at hand was a shirtless child, his ribs displayed beneath its tightly drawn skin, sucking a
piece of melon. He was playing distractedly with
the end of his father's turban, for the man lay in
the roadway, prostrated by a gunshot wound.

I had given orders that the city should be be-
flagged, and I could see hundreds of pennants
fluttering in the breeze. Thousands of stalwart
warriors had trekked down from the Kohistan
highlands, and hundreds were arriving, even as I
scanned the streets. They came, thirsty, and
tired, yet joyous, eagerly looking forward to the
gaiety and the feasting which their Bacha had
promised them.

They came singly, in twos and threes, and in
hordes, some on foot, others on Turkestan drome-
daries, still more on hardy pack ponies. There were

even those who did not despise the dwarfed hill donkey.

Rustic women, in their long, trailing robes of many colours, trailed behind the pack animals, and I could see them shout ever anon to their lordly menfolk. There would be a brief halt, and pro-testingly, the men would secure the sacks of dried fruit which they had come to trade, or refasten the cords to the legs of the fowls which hung, suspended downward, from the luggage ropes of the donkeys' packs.

I hurriedly donned an old sheep-skin coat, and went to mingle with the throng, for my heart went out to these simple folk, and I envied them their care-free existence. They did not have a coldly appraising wife of calculatingly hostile mien con-tinually to find fault. When the women down in the bazaars spoke to their men it was not: "You should not do that. It is unseemly to do this," but: "Abdul! Tie the legs of the chickens," or: "Loosen at this girth." And, a man could under-stand that.

I sallied forth. A maiden aunt from the hills was regaling her young nephews with tales of valour, looking over her shoulder meanwhile, at the Arg. She had halted by the wayside and had made a small fire, and she handed cup after cup of green tea to the youngsters. She puffed and blew at the samovar to keep the water boiling, and she told the boys that none of their clan ever died under a warm quilt. I thought of that with which I now had to contend in the palace. I buried my nose deep in the sheep-skin and smelled of its ripe aroma.

It was a skin which had warmed me on many a hillside, and deep within the wool there were splotches of dried blood. I sighed.

I paraded the city, amused with what I saw, for nearly forty thousand souls had come from the surrounding country, and the place was alive with humanity. The men, women and children lay on their bundles by the wayside, for all the serais were full. They made awnings with their homespun blankets, and I knew how snug they were. Many a time and oft, I had done the same. Now there was a woman who would array me in silk shirts and who would do me the indignity of ordering my servants to scent the water with which I bathed.

Later, when these people had rested, they marched in batches and in droves, in one mad confusion toward the Royal gardens in the lap of the encircling Kabul hills, where I had ordered that a series of contests take place. There was tent-pegging whereat the young men could display their skill upon horseback; and there was rifle shooting, and wrestling.

Unknown to the multitude, and well concealed by my sheep-skin, I entered for the tent pegging, and secured one of my own prizes. In truth I rode with vigour and there was a certain seething anger within me which I found inexplicable. Perhaps I hungered for the simple ways of the road.

After the wrestling there were inter-clan contests when young men from the hills leaped into the arena and whirled and danced to the music of the flute and the beat of the tom-toms. They jumped and turned with tremendous speed amidst the vociferous exhortations of their adherents, slashing the air with their long Afghan blades, battling one with another. It was an inspiring spectacle, and it made the blood course hotly through my veins.

Then there followed a military parade wherein all who had taken part in my victorious marches showed themselves to the populace, and men marked that the King was not present.

From amidst the seething ranks of the Kohistanis a voice was raised for the King, and the cry was taken up. There was a bustling from their centre, and a sheep-skin urged its way forward.

There was a shout as I stepped out from the multitude on to the maidan, the Kohistanis exclaiming: "The King—the King, he was with us!"

There was joy on the countenances of these simple folk, but there were those among the notables who looked down their noses when they beheld the raiment which clothed their ruler. But for that I would have cast it aside, and displayed the uniform which it hid, but I retained my mark of the hillman, and flaunted it in their faces.

I marched out about eighty yards on to the maidan toward my parading troops, and turned to address the people. The sun was behind me, and in the eyes of those who gave me acclaim. It was a fortuitous circumstance, and one which was not pre-arranged. Methinks my Mullah of the Khyber was still in good health.

As I surveyed the people thus, I discerned a sharp, flashing movement. Away toward the flank, a rifle was levelled, and it was pointed at the King. Then did the multitude see how quickly their monarch could deal with danger. My automatic rifle was in my left hand, and I did not even take the trouble to sight. A bullet winged its way beside my astrachan cap, for this would-be assassin had his weapon poised before I had seen his purpose. But the first of my shots must have crashed into his body even as his finger lugged on his trigger, for an Afghan does not so easily miss a sitting target. Five or six rounds I pumped into him before he swayed and fell amidst the crowd, and not one of my bullets harmed those about him. That was excellent shooting, and I was pleased.

The man had provided me with an element of drama which was required to round off this excellent day. He gave a fillip to my enjoyment, and the people remarked how merry was the King.

Of another incident I must recount for it concerns a game of chess, or rather several games of chess. There was one of the high-borns who was of my entourage, and the man had a melon for a head, so full was it of his own self-esteem. I discovered, quite by chance, that I could beat this individual at chess, but he never guessed that this was the true reason for his preferment. This man, accustomed to the ways of courts, should have known better, but he could never forget that his King was the son of a water-carrier, and played accordingly.

"May thy grandsires be burned alive," I was constrained to swear on more than one occasion. "You so far forget yourself as to defeat me at chess!"

And this man, instead of being contrite, would allow his eyes to gleam, and he would preen himself, for he was an exquisite in dress.

Sitting there upon the dais I would punish this man, but for long the means of blackening his face eluded me. Of course, I could have removed it altogether, but I would employ means which would burn at his high-born pride rather than cause him bodily hurt. Then, in a flash, the plan came to me, for every man has his weakness. His was an insatiable desire for a continuous sequence of new wives, and I resolved to provide him with one of surpassing beauty; but one who will give him a lasting lesson. I married him with a Mohammed Zai woman; one hailing from the clan of Amir Abdur Rahman Khan; and as I left the wedding feast I laughed in my beard, for the sour tongue of the women of that clan are hell to a man in this side of the grave.

CHAPTER XIX

NEWS FROM THE FRONTIER

THESE, my moments of leisure, I could ill-afford from the cares of State. On the one hand I had to concentrate on a steady flow of funds into the Treasury, and there were many who proved recalcitrant. Several hundred persons had necessarily to meet their deaths before the people began to realise that when their King asked for money, it was for him to receive.

Fortunately, at this time, there came to my ears an old story, for which I could find little substantiation, respecting a hidden hoard laid down by the Ameer Abdur Rahman. This Ameer always believed in having a secret reserve, and none other than he knew where this bullion lay hidden.

I suspected that Amanullah Khan had searched for this hoard while he was in the Arg. He had had ten years to devote to his task, and it was improbable, if he had failed, that I should be successful.

With a few trusted men I spent many weary hours in the dungeons beneath the Arg, and then one day I stumbled across the secret. There was indeed gold and silver there, and judging by the disarray of the treasure chamber, Amanullah had not entirely wasted his efforts.

But for this unexpected stroke of good fortune it would have been exceedingly difficult for me at periods to maintain the pay of my soldiery, but even in the leanest times I did not forget the example set up by the Ameer Abdur Rahman. I, too, would have a secret hoard, and many a night, gold and silver, packed in sacks, left on the backs of camels for the Valley of Punjshair, a little-known lair of mine in Kohistan. There, tucked away among the glens, is a considerable fortune, and the spot may be recognised by the sign of the four camels. As, however, the vultures have been at work, it is doubtful whether any marauder could find his way to this cache. I, too, took other precautions. The men who were in my confidence in the Arg have gone. The camel drivers who transported this wealth have died. The secret is mine.

This, as I say, was upon the one hand. On the other I had to do my utmost to consolidate my position among those men of position and experience who could assist me in the government of the State. In the main I made overtures to those who had been selected by the ex-King for ill-treatment, and amongst these I numbered the relatives of Nadir Khan, Amanullah's one-time Commander-in-Chief who, at the time of the revolution, was reclining upon a sick bed in Europe. I was aware that all of this family were held in the greatest esteem by the people, and that could I secure their allegiance I could snap my fingers at the rest, and see my government established upon a sound basis.

Of this family, I singled out Sardar Shah Mahmud Khan and requested him to proceed to the south, there to use his family influence in winning over the tribes to my banner. But, Sardar Shah Mahmud

Khan, when he reached the south, instead of extolling me, described me as a national calamity. It was while he was engaged in undermining me with the southern tribes that news came of the sudden arrival on the Frontier of Nadir Khan himself who, although still very ill, had decided to return to his native land. I then had no inkling of his purpose, but as Nadir Khan was entirely without financial means and was an invalid withal, I did not regard his presence as a threat to my realm. Sardar Shah Mahmud Khan immediately left for British territory, and at Parahinar, he met his brother Nadir Khan, and others of his family.

Nadir Khan, however, did not leave me long in doubt as to his purpose. He expressed his intention of driving me from the throne. This, however, was more easily said than done. I was in possession; I had the means of securing money; I had a plentiful supply of arms and ammunition; the army was contented and well-paid, and moreover, there were many members of Nadir Khan's family in Kabul. In order to be on the safe side and to curb this man's ardour, I had them all rounded up and incarcerated in the Arg.

Nadir Khan made an astute move. He made his way into Afghanistan by way of Khost where his successful tactics against the British which, in 1919 culminated in the capture of Thal, were not so readily forgotten. One regiment turned out and accorded him the Royal salute of thirty-one guns, and the tribesmen met him with bands and arranged national dances and treated the day as one of festivity.

However, there was more than one way to counter an offensive such as this. Nadir Khan's address to the tribesmen gave me the clue. He refused at that time to regard himself as the Pretender to the Throne. He said that when he had driven me out there should be a National Assembly, and a King should be elected by the vote of the people. It was not difficult in such circumstances for my emissaries to assure the people that Nadir Khan was still an officer of the late regime and that he was only stirring up trouble in an endeavour to make way for the return of Amanullah.

This proved to be most excellent propaganda, and wherever Nadir Khan rode he was met with this criticism. He was never entirely able to eradicate this unpleasant thought from the minds of the tribesmen.

Nevertheless, I lost no time in sending forces against Nadir Khan, for it was desirable to nip this movement in the bud while the General still lacked men and money. And money, I knew would prove to be an almost insurmountable difficulty. Indeed, when he stepped over the border, he was penniless, and could not even feed those who flocked to him. All he had to trade was his prestige, which was undoubtedly great, and for the rest he had to trust to luck.

I made, too, a great endeavour to win Nadir Khan to my side, for with such a man in my train, I could have been a dominating force. I sent him a message, telling him that I had had to incarcerate the members of his family, but that they would be immediately released, and he could expect the

highest honours, were he to make his way forthwith to Kabul and make submission.

The reply did not please me. It was that he could
have no intercourse with a brigand and a tyrant.

Nevertheless, I did not despair. Nadir Khan was
without money, and secretly I despatched to him
a lac of rupees. This, too, he returned, even though
I knew that at the moment he was hard put to
it to find food.

However, I intensified my propaganda regarding
the General's intrigue on behalf of Amanullah, and
so bitter was the feeling against the ex-King that
Nadir Khan found plenty of the tribesmen only
too anxious to bar his progress. Also, he was operat-
ing in an area where tribal jealousies were rampant.
Every step he took was attended by danger, and in
truth, there seemed to be little to be apprehended
from this quarter.

I relied a great deal on these tribal jealousies.
The General was early involved in a dispute between
the Wazirs and the tribes of the south. A number
of men, several thousands strong, had banded themselves together in lashkars, and declared that they
would support Nadir Khan when the Waziris of
Khost, who were refugees from their own lands of
Waziristan, fell foul of their neighbours. There had
never been much love lost between the refugees and
the men of Khost, and the latter would have them
depart. "Go, or prepare for war," they said. The
southern tribes had always regarded these men as
interlopers, and would drive them out. Both sides
armed, and if there had been a clash, that would
have been the end of Nadir Khan, but he prevailed

upon the Wazirs to take an amicable view of the situation, and both forces agreed to co-operate. Had a single bullet been fired on that occasion, the whole of the border tribes would have rushed to the aid of the Wazirs, and the General would have been ungulfed in the maelstrom.

These things are little things, but they mean much in the way of Kings.

Within a fortnight of his arrival on Afghan soil, my information was that the General had succeeded in gathering together a considerable force composed of men of many tribes, but even in this I saw no cause for alarm. Daily there would come to me stories of faction fights between these men who expended what little ammunition they had on internecine strife and seemed bent upon destroying themselves rather than the King they still termed the son of the water-carrier.

Also, it was one thing to gather together a force in a territory which was largely sympathetic toward the Nadir Khan family. It was another thing to move beyond this sphere of influence. No matter in what direction the General cared to gaze he could see in the distance terrain where the tribesmen, firm in the belief that the General had resolved to fight for the return of Amanullah, would dispute every foot of the way.

I was told that the General would march on Gardez, which is to the eastward of Ghazni, on the Kabul road, where Amanullah received his final quietus. He had to select a route which would avoid hostile territory, and this was almost impossible. But, knowing how Nadir Khan had appeared out of the blue and had taken Thal in 1919, I did not put this task beyond him.

However, I awaited impatiently in Kabul for that internal explosion which would destroy his forces, and incinerate all his plans. On the night he decided to march to Gardez by circuitous ways, there was the requisite spark. His camp was alarmed by the sudden firing of rifles from all sides. The Mangal and the Sabari tribesmen, who had long-standing enmity, and who composed the major part of his force, had decided to fight the matter out. There should have been an explosion; there was only a mis-fire. Nadir Khan persuaded these men to forget their differences, at least temporarily.

When all was ready, and the force was on the point of marching, further firing broke out. This time two sections of the Jadran clan were at each other's throats. There was considerable bloodshed, but again the fight fizzled out.

Yet, what could a commander even of the capabilities of Nadir Khan, hope to accomplish with such a rabble? Although I never under-estimated this man's military qualities, I could afford to despise the ill-armed, unpaid ruffians who would oppose me.

Nadir Khan had only fifty miles to traverse in order to reach Gardez, but his difficulties were such that the journey took him seventeen days. Even though his way was circuitous, he could not avoid the attentions of my spies who were ever before him rendering hostile tribesmen even more belli-gerent. Every step of his way was barred by men who accused him of bolstering up the cause of

Amanullah. The General had pamphlets printed and distributed in which he declared that he was not fighting for the ex-King, but the tribesmen found it difficult to assimilate this intelligence. For the main part they did not deny him passage by force of arms, but they would not provide him with food or assistance.

Eventually the General was brought to a full stop by the action of the Dari-Khels who were under the dominance of one Levannai, to whom I had sent much money. For three days and nights the General harangued deputations of the Dari-Khels who obstinately refused to believe that he was not a partisan of Amanullah.

It was here that the General resorted to force for the first time in his campaign. There were many hours of desperate fighting when Nadir Khan determined to proceed on his way, but eventually the General won through. It was, however, only with the expenditure of much ammunition which he could ill spare, and at the loss of many of his men.

The Governor of Gardez was, of course, a servant of mine. His name was Mohammad Sidiq, and he had made all preparations appropriately to receive Nadir Khan should he succeed in winning his way through the hills. When, on the seventeenth day of his march, the General was seen in the distance, he made haste to put the fort in a state of defence, but Nadir Khan did not advance to the attack. Instead, he sat down in the village of Baladeh, three miles from Gardez. Unknowing to the Governor, one of the General's brothers succeeded in making his way into the town under cover of night, and in winning over some of the principal inhabitants. Mohammad Sidiq suddenly found himself in custody, and hauled before Nadir Khan. Even as a prisoner he did his work, however. He saw what a heterogeneous host it was that the General had called together, and his barbed tongue lashed the rival tribes.

That night there was the long-expected clash. A terrific fire broke out from all quarters, and had as its objective the headquarters of Nadir Khan. The entire camp was in a panic, and the firing which ensued was wild and unaimed. Thousands of rounds were expended, and it was an hour before quiet could be restored. Hundreds met their deaths in this nocturnal encounter, but Nadir Khan and his brothers mysteriously survived.

And, he took Gardez.

CHAPTER XX

A WHISPER FROM THE KHYBER

I MARSHALLED an army of ten thousand men to deal with this menace at Gardez. As far as possible I massed this force secretly, for it was my purpose to take Nadir Khan by surprise. Another force I despatched to deal with Sardar Shah Mahmud Khan, Nadir Khan's brother, whom I had sent to the south to win over the tribes on my behalf.

I had plenty of mechanised transport at my disposal, and I was resolved to make a sudden and lightning-like thrust at Gardez, for my information was that Nadir Khan's armaments consisted of no more than two rather antiquated guns, four machine-guns, a quantity of rifles, and—eleven boxes of ammunition.

News was secretly brought to me that the General had left Gardez, and with his lashkar, had marched toward Logar, which is in a direct line with Gardez and Kabul and in the midst of the territory of the Verdaks who had always been my sternest critics and most bitter opponents.

At Dabar, the General halted, for here, in this fortified town, Pinin Beg, my advance guard commander, was in sufficient force to dispute his progress. Here, it quickly became evident that Nadir Khan intended to avoid battle if this were possible —a wise choice considering the paucity of his ammunition supplies—and he sent me a message, informing me that all the people were anxious that the question of the monarchy should be settled by the vote of a General Assembly, and suggesting that that matter be discussed. My answer was a swift courier to Pinin Beg to lose no time in taking the initiative.

The General had pushed out an advance guard two miles ahead of his lashkar, and Pinin Beg engaged this force hotly. The first news the General received of the encounter were wildly expressed appeals for more ammunition, and for men to support. There was no alternative for Nadir Khan but to join battle, and the first real encounter of the campaign was staged. It should have been the last, for I was fully prepared, and there seemed to be no avenue by which the General could escape.

The fighting proceeded throughout that day, and far into the night. The next morning, so I was informed by my intelligence, the General himself was in the firing line, personally superintending the laying of one of his two pieces of artillery on the towers of Dabar. From all accounts, the General was a pretty shot, for his shells demolished more than one of the towers, and my men had to fall back. Nadir Khan secured a temporary footing in the places which had to be evacuated. Much of the fighting was at the bayonet point, and with swords, and each side pressed home their local attacks with gallantry and vigour. For my part, I had no reason to complain of the manner in which my well paid men upheld my prestige. At noon, however, Pinin Beg received reinforcements, including a number of guns. These latter were laid on the points where the General's men had obtained a hold, and the position was speedily rendered untenable. On all points of the battle front, my men once again secured the offensive.

Following the recapture of the towers, and the tactical retirement of the General's line, there ensued a pause in the battle while both sides redisposed their forces. Suddenly, Pinin Beg saw the whole of the General's lashkar advancing in one mad rush. This attack was pressed home with such force and and such tenacity, that the ground which Nadir Khan had been forced to render up was retaken, and it was my men who were forced back.

Then, the inevitable had to happen.

On all sides within the General's ranks could be heard the insistent cry for ammunition, and more ammunition. Unfortunately, word of this was not conveyed to Pinin Beg until later—until, indeed, night had again fallen and both forces, which had been at arms for more than forty hours, sought a respite by mutual consent.

During the night, General Nadir Khan was able to replenish his supplies by purchases amongst the local tribesmen, but when dawn came the Ahmadzai section of the General's lashkar had had enough, and was dispersing in all directions. Some of these men had already crossed the local passes when light broke to reveal their defection. Soon it was clear that this lashkar was genuinely in retreat, and numbers of the local clans who had rested on the hillsides, interested spectators of the battle, decided that their moment, too, had come. They descended from their eminences and fell upon the retreating tribesmen, slaying right and left, and spoiling the dead of their arms and effects.

General Nadir Khan made an attempt to stem the rout, but a dispersal of this character, once initiated, is difficult to arrest, and before the morning was many hours old, the entire battlefield was in confusion, and Nadir Khan was left with but a mere handful of men. He was practically surrounded, and all seemed over except the shouting, yet he was enabled to steal away. He reached the Altamoor Pass in safety, even though he was hotly pursued, and from there proceeded to Sijinak, well to the eastward where once again he found himself among his sympathisers of Khost.

While this battle was proceeding, the General's brother, Sardar Shah Mahmud Khan, was hurrying to his assistance by a different route. The Sardar fell upon Khushni on his way, and a large quantity of arms and ammunition thereby fell into his hands. If only he could have made contact with his brother, the story might have been vastly different, and it might well have been that I would have been the one to be routed at Dabar. But, no sooner had the Sardar left Khushni than my reinforcements arrived at the fort. More or less at the same time came the news of the debacle at Dabar. The Sardar, halted in his tracks, turned, and would have returned to Khushni in a desperate gamble to occupy the place, but his lashkars, too, became disheartened and melted away. He also was compelled to seek little known passes. With a mere handful of men, he eventually succeeded in rejoining his brother in Khost.

I had shown the world that I could fight and defeat a General whose military attainments I had always respected and had always admired. I was well content, for the position as far as Nadir Khan was concerned was little less than desperate. For him to initiate a fresh thrust for Kabul appeared entirely out of the question, for I was in overwhelming strength everywhere, and the tribes who had supported the General were dispirited, and far from eager to try conclusions with a King who could command the moneybags.

Again I resolved to make an attempt to win the General over to my side, and for this purpose I enlisted the services of one Abdul Latif, a native of Thal, who had made Afghanistan his home, and whose inbred guile had been useful to me on more than one occasion.

I had displayed the greatest kindness to this man Latif, and he was favoured at my court, but he was a swashbuckler who had to be treated with caution. He was a surly devil on occasion, but I restrained the itching in my trigger finger because the rascal had his gifts, and could be relied upon to obtain the advantage in any bargain in which he was interested.

When I informed him that I required him to proceed to the south and interview Nadir Khan, he proved contumacious. I was unaware of the fact then, else I would have selected some other emissary, but there had been some underhand work when General Nadir Khan was marching up this fellow's native Thal in 1919 and he did not altogether relish a meeting with the General.

When I told him to prepare for his journey, Latif remained seated, and his mien was dark.

"Abdul Latif," I exclaimed angrily, "I address you. Are you deaf?"

"I am not so afflicted, Oh Bacha," he retorted. He was the only one within the court circle who still addressed me thus, but his manner was now intolerable, and aggressively supercilious.

"Son of a dog," I barked. "Know you not that your King commands you?"

The man rose slowly, and his very attitude oozed defiance and disdain. I could hear the gasps of astonishment and apprehension from my courtiers as they lined the audience chamber.

"I have other matters demanding my attention," he said with an obvious sneer. "Let some other person repair to the south and interview this General."

I had allowed this scum of the Thal sewers much license in the past, for his evil ways and open chicanery had amused me, but this was too much. The fellow was presuming. He knew, too, of the camels which secretly bore gold and silver from the Arg to my cache in Kohistan, but for all his guile, he was unaware of its location. He believed that he had this knowledge, but he was mistaken. In this he considered that he had a hold over me.

"The order has been given, Abdul Latif," I remarked coldly, in an endeavour to hide my rage. "You will depart at once. I will have a motor car prepared."

"I do not wish to meet Nadir Khan," he said, still insolently. "Are there not others here who can perform this task? Are those about you afraid to meet this soldier face to face?"

He leered up at me.

"Why does not Bacha perform this service for the nation? Is he too afraid of peering into the eyes of Nadir Khan?"

I glared into the eyes of this ingrate, and my finger on the trigger of my automatic rifle twitched with the urgency which was within it. But I threw it aside with an oath.

"Afraid," I yelled. "I, your King, afraid! I am afraid of no man, not even of Abdul Latif!"

I descended from the dais, and drew my sword.

I called to the guards round the audience chamber.

"Make a ring," I cried. "Make a ring, and give this man a sword. We will fight. It should be a good fight, for one or the other of us will die."

The soldiers formed a ring, and a sword was thrust into the hands of Abdul Latif. I threw myself on guard, and I gazed into the eyes of this upstart. I could have laughed aloud at what I saw. His gaze drooped, and he looked uncomprehendingly at the weapon with which he was armed. He liked not the task which was before him.

"On guard!" I cried. "On guard, or I skewer you."

Still he allowed his sword to droop.

"Oh valiant one from the land of the Ferenghi," I sneered. "Up with your sword," and I pricked him lightly on the shoulder. He squirmed, and looked around the circle of grinning faces.

I pricked him again, and he turned, but there was no escape out of that ring. I prodded him from behind, and he commenced to run, and once, twice, thrice, I pricked his wobbling buttocks.

At last, with a cry of anguish, he succeeded in forcing a way through the convulsed guards, but I had him brought back.

"What now, Abdul Latif," I said. "Do you go to Khost?"

"I do, sire," he replied humbly enough.

I called the Court Chamberlain.

"Cancel the order for the Rolls," I said, "and have prepared one of the Fords from the transport lines. Select, if possible, one which is deficient in springs and is devoid of cushions. This Abdul Latif shall remember his journey."

I had every reason to believe that he did.

In my message to Nadir Khan, I asked the General to give up the fight, and to send in his allegiance. I, on my part, promised him any post he liked to name, and to return all his lands and property. Failing this, I threatened to put to death all the members of his family in Kabul. As I had sixty-one of them safely in the Arg, I considered this final appeal to be all compelling.

I also told the General, that if there was any question of casting lots for the throne, this could be done easily enough in Kabul.

There was a nasty smirk on Abdul Latif's face when he returned, and for once I regretted my inability to read. As was my custom, however, I had the General's missive read aloud in the audience chamber. I swore loudly as the pages were unfolded.

"To Habibullah, the son of the water-carrier," this message started. Except to give me the title which I had assumed, there was no reference to my Kingship, and only this insistence upon my lowly origin.

"I received your message and the offer it contained," the letter proceeded. "It seems to me that you are quite ignorant of my purpose and my intentions, and that your counsellors too have misguided you in this respect.

"My object in returning to my Motherland at such a time is neither to have the throne, nor to share it with you.

"I have come here simply to do away with internal unrest, and put an end to this bloody civil war which is corroding the foundation of the nation. This national catastrophe has been brought about by you. Although, because of your ignorance, you do not realise the damage you have done to the nation, yet the sensible world lays all the blame at your door, and the day of reckoning is not far. Myself and my companions wish to see Afghanistan enjoying peace and prosperity. This is my goal, and whoever crosses my path, I would look upon as a national enemy, and would do my best to remove him from my way.

"A few days ago I sent you a message. It was clearly pointed out to you that as long as you held the reins of Government, it was impossible to see peace in the country. You were, therefore, called upon to retire. You had the audacity to refuse.

Even now I am willing to give you a chance, for I have come for peace, and have no desire to shed blood. Nothing would give me greater pleasure than to restore peace in the country, without recourse to arms. But, I am sure that so long as an ignorant person like you remains on the throne, the nation cannot enjoy peace or happiness.

"You are not fit for the responsibility which you have assumed, and no one is willing to accept you as King. I, therefore, once more advise you to vacate the throne, and allow the people to have a King of their own choice. If, however, you are obstinate and crazy about the throne, you will only be aggravating the existing troubles, and I will be compelled to fight you until the last.

"Regarding your threats to kill my relatives who are now in Kabul in case I refuse to accept your sovereignty, let me tell you frankly that again you misjudge me. If in the cause of the national welfare I were to lose all my relatives, or even my own life, I would feel proud of such a noble sacrifice.

"Remember, O tyrant——"

I held up my hand, and called upon the reader to desist. This was enough.

This was the answer from a man who had been defeated in battle, had narrowly escaped with his life, and to whom all honour had been accorded.

I raved and I swore, for the missive was abusive, and poured scorn upon my pretensions to the throne. Pretensions indeed! Had I not taken Kabul by force of arms? Had I not held the country in the face of armed insurrection? Had I not proved to be myself a King.

I called angrily to those who were chattering lightly around the walls. I bade them hold their tongues. I did more, I ordered them to depart. I would be alone. I had nothing to fear from this man tucked away amongst his friends in Khost, but I liked not the taste of his missive.

I reclined heavily upon a pile of cushions, my mind toying with schemes of vengeance, for I would be repaid for the insults which had been poured upon me.

There were all these people in the Arg. Should I take this Nadir Khan at his word, have these people paraded before me, and have an afternoon's pleasurable blood-letting? It would be good to see these people die—this family which would throw scorn upon the son of a water-carrier.

I allowed the thought to revolve in my mind. It brought the saliva to my mouth as I schemed and schemed and worked out the details of each individual passing. This Nadir Khan said it would be an honour. Well, he should have honour.

As I cogitated thus, a hand came to my shoulder. I sat up in anger, for I had given orders that I was to be allowed to remain in peace.

It was Malik Mohsin, the ancient, and the droop to his pendulous lips told me that he had news to impart.

"Well," I demanded testily, "what is it? Don't tell me that you have come to tell me that the Arg prisoners have escaped!"

He shook his grey head, and mumbled in his beard.

I bade him speak up, for he could be irritating when he had tidings to convey.

"Your Mullah of the Khyber," he said hesitantly.

"Yes?"

"As you know, sire, I have always kept track of this man of prophecy. He has said so much that has come true. . . ."

"Well?"

"I am informed that he is sick and ailing."

I rose to my feet. I pulled at my beard in my exasperation.

"But," I exclaimed testily, "haven't you despatched medicines and doctors?"

"Sire," said Malik, "unknowing to you the Mullah has always had these attentions. Now I fear——"

He gazed at me, the personification of gloom.

"It is something which the hakims cannot cure," he added.

"It is age—old age. His time is not long."

CHAPTER XXI

I FIGHT FOR MY THRONE

WAS there anything in the prophecy of this Mullah?

Could it not be that I had achieved my eminence by the force of my own arms? Could it not be my own virile mind which had dictated my ascent from the village hut to the palace, and not the mere forces of Destiny?

I was sorely troubled.

In the south Nadir Khan was continuing his propaganda. He was sending missions to the various tribes, urging upon them to forget their tribal jealousies, and to unite in one supreme effort to reach Kabul. This, of course, was merely talk, and probably nothing would come of it. But, in a few weeks' time all the harvests would be garnered, and the men of the southern villages would be idle, and fair game for the astute spinner of words. It was always after the harvests that the greatest danger was to be apprehended.

Yet, when I took stock of the material situation, there was little that could spell misgiving. Nadir Khan's forces hardly existed. I had routed him in a pitched battle, and he had narrowly escaped with his life. Even Kandahar had accepted me, and as head of the Kandahar province I had Abdul Latif who, after his ignominious display in the Salam

Khana, had been only too willing to assure me of his obedience, and—incidentally, to lave his own much wounded pride by lording it over others. Abdul Latif kept me supplied with a continuous stream of informers, and there was little that happened in the south that I did not know.

For those who refused to speak when interrogated, or sought to evade the truth, I had constructed in the Arg an iron chair. Attached to the chair was an iron contrivance which held the head immovable. A barber and—irony of ironies—a water carrier did the rest.

When the silent one was in the chair, and his head was held so that he could not even wrinkle his skin, the barber would shave a small area on the top of his head. Then the water carrier would appear and fill an earthenware container attached to the roof. In the container had been bored a tiny hole, and at regular intervals, a drop of water would descend some eleven or twelve feet on to the shaved area. Always would it fall on to the same spot. A day of such treatment was usually enough. Those who were sufficiently obdurate to remain silent for two days were grey. Those who remained longer were gibbering lunatics. It was an old device, but an excellent one.

When I looked nearer at hand, however, I had to confess to some little misgivings. Money was again proving a problem, for many of the wealthy were now poor, and it was becoming increasingly difficult to secure money by means of torture. I had Malik Mohsin apply his well-known arts to the utmost, but there was no mistaking the fact that the stream of gold was dwindling. Many of the ordinary people, too, were unemployed, and the police were reporting a certain amount of rioting around the bread shops.

At this juncture, I was informed that Nadir Khan was making overtures to the trans-border tribes, and that these men, always out for loot and slaughter, had displayed a disposition to listen to him. Even here, I could find solace, for my sojourn in Peshawar had told me that these sleepy Ferenghi would put difficulties in his way. They did. The trans-border tribesmen were informed that they would not be allowed to move into Afghan territory, and here, too, the Fates seemed to be on my side.

At length, however, all the harvests were garnered, and men began to gather around the General. In August, there was some local fighting, and Nadir Khan once again sent a force to contest Gardez. The General's men appeared at the gates of this fortress without previous warning, but they were repulsed, and the battle that ensued lasted two days. My artillery continually lashed the ground, and the General's lashkars suffered heavy casualties. On the morning of the third day my reinforcements arrived on the scene, and the Gardez garrison moved out to fight the lashkars in the open. For a further forty-eight hours this battle was joined, and the fighting was fierce in the villages of Tor and Speen. Then, when it seemed that the General's forces must break, the unexpected happened. A large Wazir lashkar from across the border mysteriously appeared, and my men were forced to give up Gardez. The General took a large number of my men prisoners, and for the moment he solved the problem of his ammunition supply, for the fortress of Gardez was well stocked.

That evening, I received news from the Khyber. My Mullah was dead.

Again I was torn by doubt, and I slept little. Continuously I fingered the amulet which had never left me, and more than once my fingers gripped it.

I would toss upon my couch, and I would concentrate all my endeavours on forgetting this man, and the insignificant bangle which encircled my arm. My fingers would pierce my flesh as I tried to summon that resolve where I would tear this thing from my body. I would defy the Fates. I would laugh at this seer!

For two moons after his death, he had said. But, what was there to foretell disaster. True, Gardez had fallen, but it could soon be retaken.

Sometimes, lying there, I could have screamed in my mental anguish. There was always this doubt. It nagged at me throughout the hours of darkness, and it fogged my decisions during the day. It became an obsession. Every step I took became an effort. Every word I uttered had to be most carefully weighed. Always, behind my every action, no matter how insignificant, was the thought: What does this entail? What does this portend?

Those around me in the Arg began to notice my indecision, and it was whispered that the Mullah was dead. I flew into unaccountable rages, and I swore that before two moons had passed this General Nadir Khan should be swept from the land.

Malik Mohsin began to lose his taste for butchery, and I chided him.

"Greybeard," I taunted, "you are becoming over old for a post of such pleasure—methinks we shall have to appoint a woman. A woman always knows how to delve beneath the skin."

He mumbled in his beard, and he gazed at me with his lugubrious, rheumy eyes.

"Think a woman would spill blood as I have spilled it?"

He shook his head, and I saw that his aged hands fluttered as with the palsy.

"Bacha—sire," he said. "I am an old man—my life is nearly spent. Sometimes I see things, and—they are not pleasant."

His eyes took on an intense pleading, yet I saw that he hesitated to give utterance to his thoughts.

"Something troubles you, Malik," I prompted.

Suddenly, as if pulling up the gates of a dam, he unloosed a torrent of words.

"Bacha—forgive me for calling you that—but I claim the licence of my age. We are not men of palaces—we are not men of the cities—we cannot govern these people by slaughter alone—let us return to our hills. Let us gather our wealth, for that is our way, and return to the village fires and make merry. . . ."

Rage and resentment were within me, for I had shown this man many favours, but that pulsating doubt which was within me bade me hold my tongue.

"This is no place for us, Bacha," he went on, taking courage at my unwonted silence. "This place stinks of blood and death, and I like it not. Even the vulture and the jackal retire after the feast, and—we have had enough. Come, Bacha— the hills—movement—freedom. . . ."

"Enough, Malik," I broke in. Truly, I was afraid to trust my voice, for if Malik could think thus, what of the rest?

"You are indeed over old," I continued, "otherwise you would know that what I have I hold. I am no mere hill brigand. You forget, old man, that I am King and that you are Governor of Kabul. . . ."

He wring his hands in a helpless gesture.

"Come," I enjoined. "What of these things that you see?" I spoke pleasantly enough, but Malik shivered.

"The Mullah—the Mullah!" he muttered.

I laughed, for I would not have this old man know of my own secret forebodings.

"Surely," I cried, fingering my rifle, "you don't believe in these old women's tales?"

He remained silent.

"Do you?" I demanded, for I had been without sleep for many nights, and my nerves were on edge.

Malik dissembled.

"Sire," he mumbled weakly, "I feel sick. I am indisposed. I beg to be excused." And, salaaming, he left the audience chamber.

These vapid outpourings from a doddering ancient only made me the more determined to defy the Fates. I would take stock of the position, and act as the King I was.

I called for my horse, and with a small escort, made for a favourite retreat within the nearby hills. There, in communion with myself, I saw what was wrong. I came to myself with a start. Verily, I was taking too serious a view of incidents which might well happen to any ruler of a country such as Afghanistan.

As I lay there, in the pure mountain air, I forced myself to see myself as a detached being, and I was not pleased with the picture. There I was, a craven, torn with nerve-searing doubt, and assailed by troubled memories. I saw myself as a nervous, highly-strung incompetent—a man who was dashing headlong for a breakdown. The remedy, I could see, lay in my own hands. First I must repair the ravages of lost repose. That in itself would restore my powers of determined action and of clear thought.

I returned to the Arg, refreshed, and with my fears left upon the hillsides.

Secretly, I summoned my physician, and I told him that I would sleep. He prepared drugs from the charas, and that night, and every night thereafter, I slept. But, I still dreamed.

My difficulty in respect to General Nadir Khan was the fact that I never knew in what direction he might strike. My knowledge of his military strategy was in itself an adverse quality. I remembered how he had fooled the English in his marches on Kohat. I had reason to know how he had taken my commanders by surprise by his sudden appearance before Gardez.

The General, because of his accession of strength

following his capture of arms, provided something
of a problem. It would require a very considerable
force to seek him out and to give open battle, and
I knew enough of this soldier's capabilities not lightly
to embark upon such a course. Moreover, it was
extremely probable that if I did detach a large
body for this purpose, it would never make contact
with him, and other centres would remain unprotected.

Where the General could remain compact, I had
to extend and distribute my men, and this explains
why Nadir Khan was enabled suddenly to make
a thrust at Khushi. Khushi is in the Logar Valley,
and might be described as one of the many keys
to Kabul. It was not, however, on his direct line
of advance, and for once my intelligence did not
serve me. I had been led to suppose that if the
General moved at all, he would operate more to
the westward in an effort to secure the Ghazni-
Kabul road—a far more orthodox means of approach.

My intelligence was correct in one respect, and
that was that the General himself was not prepared
to move on Khushi. But it left out the probability
of his brother, Sardar Shah Wali Khan, being
deputed for this service, and the first intimation
I had of the movement was that Shah Wali Khan
was in possession.

Yet, even though Khushi itself was lightly held,
I had a considerable army immediately behind in
the Wagho-Jan Pass, and while I held this pass,
Kabul was safe. I did not expect Sardar Shah
Wali Khan to attack me here, but he did. He
despatched a lashkar some thousands strong to

storm the heights, and it was evening when battle became general. The fight proceeded throughout the night, and when dawn broke, my men found that the enemy had secured several heights which gave opportunities for enfilading fire. Many of my men had to yield, and they were taken, with large quantities of ammunition.

Hurriedly, I despatched reinforcements, and after bitter fighting my men succeeded in recapturing the lost heights, but in turn, Sardar Shah Wali Khan received aid, and for a further two days this battle raged, first one side, then the other, securing the advantage. I sent body after body of men into the fray, but I had to give of my men sparingly, for I knew not where the General himself would appear. In the end my men broke, and retired from the pass. Thus, almost in a night, and without any previous warning, the enemy had secured the gate to the capital.

It did not mean, however, that General Nadir Khan had defeated me. I was determined that he should not enter the capital as I had entered it, and that if he ever set foot in it he would have to fight every step of the way. I was no Amanullah. Moreover, I was not one to cower behind walls. True, I added to the fortifications of the Arg, but principally I directed my attention to increasing the weight of armaments upon the surrounding hills—upon Asmai, Sher Darwaza and Maranjan. If General Nadir Khan were resolved to try a gambit, he should meet with a hot reception.

Meanwhile, notwithstanding his statements about glory, I still had the members of his family in the

Arg, and if there was going to be any shooting, I felt that I held the trump card.

Secretly, I gave instructions for quarters to be prepared which were in the direct line of any artillery fire which might be directed upon the Arg.

If the worst came to the worst, I would have these people placed in this post of danger, and every shot which the General directed at the palace would reach an objective which he would not relish.

Moreover, if he should appear within striking distance of Kabul, I would take care to inform him of the fact. If he was anxious for battle, he should at least have a target!

CHAPTER XXII

SUSPENSE

I COULD but regard the fall of this important pass with the greatest misgivings, yet when I viewed the broad aspects of the situation, I could take heart. I had been in far worse positions, and the day was still far from lost. There was much to be done before Nadir Khan and I settled accounts, and if I played my cards aright, I still held the trump.

Yet, riding through the bazaars of Kabul, and the outlying hills, inspecting the defences, I should have been blind had I not sensed the undercurrents of suspense and excitement pervading all. Wherever I went, I saw heads furtively peering, and I could not rid my mind of the impression that the people were waiting . . . just waiting.

From the moment when General Nadir Khan had appeared on the borders, I had instilled in the minds of the Kabulis the suggestion that the General was really the agent and servant of the despised Amanullah. But, notwithstanding all my precautions, Nadir Khan had succeeded in smuggling a number of pamphlets into the capital in which he set out his true aims.

More than one man had been bastinadoed for reading aloud from these documents.

I had to take precautions. There were those in Kabul who would betray the city to the enemy if they were given the smallest opportunity.

I instituted a curfew and required all unauthorised civilians to be in their homes after nightfall. I made it a capital offence, and punishment was summary, for more than five persons to gather together in the streets during the hours of daylight.

Men who were suspected of dealing with the enemy, I had removed to the aerodrome, where a few pounds of black powder were sufficient to hurl them from the mouths of the ancient cannon, which I kept there specially for this purpose.

I was determined to make the people see that I was not to be intimidated, either by possible betrayal from within, or by the menace from without.

In point of fact, the sustained exercise, and the necessity for continuous riding, brought me pleasure. It was better to be about the walls and the outer defences, than a prey to disturbing doubts upon a couch in my apartments.

For the nonce I became the old Bacha, full of vigour and of good cheer. Those around me caught of the atmosphere, and those who had worn long faces when the pass was taken, began to take heart, and to enthuse in the preparations for the coming encounter.

The enemy were not slow to make their intentions known, and it was when the day dawned on October 8, 1929, that the first lashkars moved against the capital. This force had the Maranjan Hill as its objective, which pleased me well, for I had concentrated a number of heavy guns in the posts there, and I could offer a very hot reception.

I went to the hill myself, and superintended the fire, which was devastating. The shot ploughed great avenues through the packed ranks of the lashkars, and the slaughter was great. It was, of course, impossible for the enemy to press home its attack in the face of such a bombardment, and after some hours' fighting, I had the satisfaction of seeing the sadly mauled lashkars retire.

In all, this force made three separate and distinct attempts to carry the hill and its fortress, and on the third and last occasion, I led a charge against it. We got well home, and the enemy ranks broke. I disdained the sword, but fired with my magazine rifle as we galloped forward.

I returned to the Arg that night well content, for the people of Kabul had seen that I intended to fight, and the General's forces had had a taste of my mettle. They would now realise that if ever they were to set foot in Kabul, the way would be piled with the dead.

Word reached me next day of reinforcements rallying to the enemy, but I believed my position to be secure. Throughout the day I rode round the defences, awaiting the next onslaught.

It came that night. The lashkars which had taken part in the previous fighting for the Maranjan Hill had had their ranks filled, and again they pressed forward. Under cover of darkness they were able to avoid, to a considerable extent, the curtain of artillery fire which I laid down for their discomfiture. At length, and notwithstanding the formidable

barriers they had to surmount, the enemy lashkars
secured a footing in the outskirts of the city in the
playing fields of Chaman-i-Hazuri.

While this fight was in progress, another was
being bitterly contested on the other side of the
city. Here was the main force, under the General's
younger brother, Sardar Shah Wali Khan, and I
had every available gun turned on this mass of men.
Again, however, the darkness favoured the attackers,
and here, too, the enemy succeeded in establishing
himself. The fighting, as I have indicated, was
bitter, and time and time again I led forth sorties
against the enemy, but in the darkness and the
confusion it was frequently difficult to differentiate
between friend and foe.

In the end my men fell back, and my officials
within the city displayed their cowardice by decamp-
ing. Those whose duty it was to enforce the curfew,
and to prevent crowds of people gathering, faded
into the darkness, and as I made my way to the
Arg, I could see the populace issuing from its hiding
places, and fraternising with the advance troops of
the enemy.

From the Arg I could visualise the scene, for the
people assembled bands and beat drums, and
marched through the bazaars singing songs of
praise. Continually there were loud shouts of
"Nadir! . . . Nadir!"

I would give them Nadir!

They thought then that Kabul was taken, and
that the reign of Bacha was over, but they were
mistaken. I still held the trump card, and the
citadel had yet to be invested. As long as I held

the Arg I was still master, and master I would remain.

It was now that I made known my intentions. As soon as the gates of the palace had been closed behind me, I bade Malik Mohsin place the General's relatives in the apartments which I had provided for them. They were brought up from their quarters where they could have remained in comparative safety, and were awarded honourable positions well within the line of fire.

I then sent word to Sardar Shah Wali Khan and told him that he could inform his brother the General that every shot fired at the citadel would find its mark on one of his relatives.

That seemed to dispose of an immediate attack on the Arg, and, in truth, there was little more fighting that night. The next forenoon, too, passed without undue incident, and I remained quiescent because I was massing my men in the north under my lieutenant, Purdil.

That night (October 10) Purdil fell upon the enemy with every man I could muster. He initiated the attack from the Paghman side, and his onslaught took the General's forces by surprise.

The principal clash was centred around the old Habibia College, and I made my way there to join in the fray, for I realised that this encounter must be decisive.

In this fighting I received a slash on the arm which made me drop my rifle. I lost it in the press of jostling, cursing men, and had to have recourse to a sword. While fighting thus Purdil himself received a mortal wound, and fell at my side, and seeing this some poltroon raised a cry. He bellowed like a lost soul, and I cut my way toward him, and struck him down. But the mischief had been done. The cry was taken up. It was said that my men were dispersing, and—indeed, they were. I was left fighting alone, and savagely had I to wield my sword to carve a way clear.

Eventually, I reached the Arg, but I was exhausted.

My great counter-stroke—the one which was to rid Kabul of the enemy before Nadir Khan himself could arrive on the scene—had failed. All now depended upon the defences of the Arg, and the fact that with me within the citadel were so many whom the General would hesitate to submit to a bombardment.

There was little sleep for any of us in the Arg that night.

To add to my desolation, the lady who was my wife sought me out and reproached me for the manner in which I had disposed of the General's relatives. Her barbed attack was couched in the speech of the high-born, and her words, always difficult to counter, had been well prepared before she approached me.

"Are you," she asked in her regal way, "Habibullah the King, or Bacha the Brigand?"

I was fatigued almost beyond endurance, and I was in no mind to answer riddles.

"Why trouble me with women's chatter?" I growled from my couch. "Is the present a time to torment me and to introduce the converse of the Hareem?"

"I would," she continued, quite unabashed, "that you were Bacha the Brigand, for it was frequently said that the Bacha of old assisted those who were in distress."

Again I growled, for this woman had the gift of tongues, and when unduly tired words come to me haltingly, and ire and irritation consumes me.

"In placing these women and children in the post of danger," she went on imperturbably, "Habibullah the King is branded as a coward!"

I jumped to my feet, oaths falling from my lips, for every man has his limit of endurance. I would have struck her there and then, but though her face expressed fear, there was something in her eyes which made me hold my hand.

I stood glaring at her for two . . . three seconds, and she laughed.

"That has touched you," she said. "You think that I would heap dishonour upon you. But—I am a true woman, and I would not that my husband sully his name in this way."

"Why should I show softness to these people?" I demanded, goaded by this woman's cool air. "After all, I am the King, and I might have put them to death long since. . . ."

"You might!" she agreed.

"And if anything befalls them now, it will not be the King who will have encompassed their deaths, but Nadir Khan. He has only to restrain his fire, and they are safe. . . .

"I see that you are displeased," I went on, my irritation growing. "Yet, what might a man do in these circumstances?"

"You might return these people to a place of safety!"

"Woman," I cried in my anger, "you forget yourself. You forget that those of your sex are always meddling. You are the wife of the King, and should be content when you see him take steps that you might retain that position."

Such an argument should have felled a man but with a woman the logical only gives of greater incentive to guile.

"True," she responded, drawing herself up in her hauteur, "you have all the manliness, and also the bugle with which to blow your own fanfares."

This was too much, even from a wife.

"Impertinence such as yours," I flared, "is usually awarded by the lash."

This noble-born paled, and gazed at me incredulously.

"The lash," she repeated incredulously, "the lash? What mean you?"

"Lady," I answered, and there was more than mockery in my tone, for here was a woman prattling of that which did not concern her while her King was fighting for his throne, "I think you know. I am aware of the manner in which you keep order within your own apartments. Many a servant has complained to me, and has shown me his lacerated flesh. . . ."

"But . . . I am the Queen!" Her eyes flashed fire.

"Madam," I replied, roughly enough, "you are a woman, with a woman's tongue. How would you like the lash to curl round your undraped back?"

"Oh. This is intolerable." Her tirade made my ears sing.

At last I could stand no more, and I caught her by the shoulder.

"Enough woman. Enough!" I shouted, for I had to raise my voice to make myself heard. "Another word from you, and there will be whip cutting into you!"

She could see that my ire was raised, and that I really meant what I said.

For several seconds we stood thus, eyeing each other,—an infuriated tigress glaring at an angry tiger. Then, for the first time in our companionship, her eyes melted, and she became womanly.

"Bacha," she said softly, taking a tiny step toward me, "perhaps it is that you have played your part. Perhaps it is that you will have to leave the Arg; if you must needs go, I will come with you. I will be the wife of Bacha the Brigand. I will cook for you, and care for you. . . ."

She took another step toward me, and fondled my hand.

I think I have said that I was well nigh spent, and I cursed that this further affliction should have been put upon me. By then I knew that it might shortly be imperative for me to make my way back to my hills of Kohistan, but why should I be thus punished?

Aloud, I said.

"As you will, woman. Should it be that I return to the mountains, and to my poor abode there, be careful with my poor belongings chiefly rifles and knives, and do not disturb them unduly."

And the lady, smiling that inner smile of satisfaction which only women can achieve, made for the curtained apartments, and left me in peace.

I was resolved, if I had to leave the Arg, that this female should be apprised of my going only after I had reached the security of the mountains; for her tongue would set a haystack afire.

CHAPTER XXIII

THE BOMBARDMENT

With Malik Mohsin I discussed the position well into the night. The old man still prattled of the Mullah, and regarded all as lost. It was in vain that I endeavoured to flog into life his fading hopes. He was convinced that the hour had come and that the reign of Habibullah was at an end.

I had long passed the stage when I could sustain anger, for sleep and repose had long been denied me. And in Malik Mohsin I had one who must necessarily remain by my person, because of the energy with which he had pursued his duties as Governor of Kabul.

Ever anon, through the night watches, we could hear the shouts of the populace, and punctuating the plaudits for Nadir Khan could be heard the demands for the person of the Governor. The people would have Malik Mohsin to have their vengeance on him. As he listened, the old man shivered.

"Thy people, they shout for thee, Malik," I remarked to him, for I could not deny myself the pleasantry. "What it is to be popular in the face of the multitude!"

He turned a grey face to me, wet with moisture, and his words were indicative of his thoughts, for no longer did he address me as King.

"Bacha," he said tremulously, "we must be away. Soon Nadir Khan will join his brother, and there will be no way from the Arg."

I scoffed at the suggestion.

"Think you," I jeered, "that the General will kill his own women and children?"

Malik shrugged his shoulders. He was distraught, and miserable, and ached for the smell of his hill-sides. He glanced apprehensively around the walls of the Salam Khana. Again he heard the people shouting his name, and he turned bloodshot eyes to mine.

I turned on him with irritation. "You do every-thing except squeal," I flung at him. "You drift around like some caged jackal, seeking a means of escape."

"Escape, yes!" he muttered. "Can't you hear them, Bacha? Can't you hear them?"

"Errh! You disgust me, Malik." And, indeed the old man was a contemptible figure. "The good citizens only desire to honour you, and to return of your hospitality. They would take you to the aerodrome, and hoist you upon one of those posts. Then, they would let you drop, as you have dropped hundreds, Malik, and they would converse sweetly with you as you sat there, impaled."

The old man's eyes flashed fire for a moment, and his dignity returned to him.

"You know what would happen to you, Bacha, should they take you?"

I laughed, for the prospect did not alarm me.

"I should look down the muzzles of a firing squad, perhaps."

"Firing squad!" Malik was sarcastic. "They reserve such a death for soldiers and Kings. Perhaps they would regard you as a robber, and place you in one of those cages to starve to death."

"Perhaps," I jeered, "but they have yet to take me, and—the Arg."

It was while Malik and I were thus wrangling, that a courier made his way to me. He had been in the enemy's lines, and he brought word of a message which had been delivered to Sardar Shah Wali Khan from his brother, the General.

In this letter, Nadir Khan ordered his brother to commence bombarding the Arg immediately. "In this hour of crisis," he wrote, "the choice lies between the safety of the nation and the safety of my relatives. Bombard, therefore, without the slightest consideration of our dear ones."

I confess that I was amazed when the contents of this letter were made known to me, and I questioned and cross-questioned the messenger. He protested that there could be no room for doubt, and that confirmation would come with the dawn, when Sardar Shah Wali Khan was determined to open with his guns.

Never for one moment had I believed that the General would make such a sacrifice, and the news stunned me. I knew then that the Mullah was a true seer. Nevertheless, I would fight it out to the last. There was many a slip 'twixt cup and lip, and I had emerged from tighter corners than this.

As my messenger predicted, with the dawn of October 2 came the ominous rumble of the enemy guns and the first shells crashed into the citadel.

With those preliminary shots all shadow of doubt was removed, and I thought of the sarcastic barbs hurled at me by my lady wife. Secretly, I gave orders for the removal of Nadir Khan's children and womenfolk from their positions of danger. The males I had remain as a sop to my vanity. Yet, none except a very few were aware of what I had done. I was resolved that those directing the firing from Kabul's outskirts should have full measure of suspense and mental unease. To add to their qualms, I returned round for round, and throughout that day the artillery duel was maintained.

Many times the enemy massed for the attack, but on each occasion, the guns of the citadel broke up the formation, and they were compelled to fall back.

No, I was a fighter, and I would not give up without a struggle that which I had won.

The next day the bombardment began afresh, and it was now that the walls began to show signs of the terrific battery to which they had been subjected. A breach was slowly pounded in one part, and I knew then that an assault in force could not be long delayed.

As the day wore on, the situation became worse, and the magazine caught fire. Many shells went off with a terrific detonation, and the fire spread.

I could see that the garrison was losing heart, but I went round the walls, insisting that all rounds by each gun should be fired, yet as soon as I departed to a further redoubt my ears told me that more and more pieces were falling silent, and that my gunners were fading away.

By continuously patrolling the ramparts, however, I was enabled to maintain some semblance of resistance, and sundry of my guns were still spouting when darkness fell.

But it was the end. Of that there could be no shadow of doubt.

The reign of Habibullah was over. Would it be that that of Bacha the Brigand would have another lease?

Hastily I denuded the Treasury of that which was easily portable, but transport proved a difficulty. We had to make for the hills, Malik and I, and a Rolls would not serve our purpose.

At length I decided that two camels would meet the occasion. There were thousands of camels around the city brought in by the lashkars, and two more would not be noticed. Moreover, no one would look for Bacha upon these slow-moving beasts.

Just before midnight on October 2, Malik and I slipped through the breach, and Habibullah had ceased to be.

Instead, once more free for action, and out again on the prowl, was Bacha, the water-carrier's son.

But these camels! Indeed were they daughters of Shaitan. Neither was muzzled, and they bore a deep antipathy one of the other.

Five miles from Kabul we halted, for both Malik and I were exhausted before we began our march, and we had spent over four hours in covering the distance. Such was our fatigue that we forgot the camels, and they were at each other like fiends from hell.

Have you ever seen camels fight? No! 'Tis not

a pretty sight. These were pack animals, and not the sweet-breath trotting variety, and their abhorrent, green-hued, disease-laden teeth closed and tore great hunches of hair and flesh. Both animals shrieked and screamed in their rage and their agony, for here, too, was a fight to the death, and the noise of the combat drew attention. We had necessarily to leave them to their duel, and seek the shelter of the boulders, and the sanctuary of the darkness.

We could hear people running, and it was with great difficulty that we avoided discovery.

Shots rang out, and the camels fell. There was a short interval during which we could see prying hands at work upon the budnles which cloaked the treasure. Then a great hubbub arose, and the cry of:

"The Bacha. . . . The Bacha! . . . The Bacha is here. . . . Come, let us take him, for the reward will be many squares of land!"

Malik and I crawled on our bellies like snakes, and we were free.

When dawn came, both of us, more dead than alive, could see a village in the distance, and clumps of mulberry trees in the valley below. Beyond an occasional bark from the village dogs, and the cries of the women who carried their water pitchers to their homes from the adjoining wells, the place was lifeless. Here we were in a tract which had always been hostile to me, and the men were with Nadir Khan.

Yet neither of us could make a move. Hungry and thirsty, we dared not make a descent upon the village, even though it be peopled only by women.

Rather would I have had the men there, for men fight clean. These hill women, when they take to the sword, as they will in the absence of their men-folk, resort to ways which would make a man blush and shamed. They have no sense or appreciation of the male dignity, and they are genuinely and avowedly sadistic.

All we could do was to curse, suck pebbles, and take it in turns to snatch a few hours' sleep.

For three days we wandered among the hillsides, drinking of the water of the streams, and tightening the cords of our pyjamas, for there was no place where we might eat.

At length, beyond the compass of the outer ranges, we reached the hills of Kohistan, and at our feet lay another village. We stumbled down a rocky goat track, and went forward with renewed hope, for here I was among my people, and would receive succour.

As we walked along there emerged from behind a mass of scrub a tall highlander. He had a rifle in his hands, and he bade us halt.

"Stand," he cried, "or your wives are widows!"

We stood.

"Who are you?" he demanded roughly.

"Who but Habibullah, your King," I answered sourly, for this man should have recognised me as a friend.

He started, and peered intently at my ravaged features.

"Bacha!" he breathed, but I looked in vain for the broadening grin which would presage good fellowship, and the killing of goats.

He stood there, his rifle ready for action, as if he suspected my motives. He radiated unease.

"We of this village would have none of Bacha," he said, and he gazed into the distance to the hills over which we had passed. My eyes followed his gaze, and I understood.

There was movement there, and I guessed that we were being trailed.

"Nadir Khan has been proclaimed King these three days," he continued gruffly, "and there have been soldiers here whose orders are to arrest you at all costs. . . ."

"And you would have nothing of Bacha?" The man caught the sarcastic inflection, and had the grace to appear abashed.

"You would forget the way of the hills, and deny the traveller food and shelter?"

The man hesitated.

"We want none of Bacha," he reiterated. "All have paid homage to the new King for he is all powerful. But . . . stay . . . I will return to the village and obtain bread. Thereafter, you must go."

Thus it was that we broke our fast, Malik and I, out on the hillsides, tearing apart of the sour pancakes. It was rough fare, and came ill after nine months of plenty in the Arg, but we heaped blessings upon the surly wretch who undoubtedly saved our lives. Yet he could not have offered this provender with more ill-grace.

"Begone," he muttered as he handed over the brown cakes. "Begone, Bacha, and you too, Malik Mohsin, for there is evil in your train."

The manner of this reception cast a gloom over us, but I found solace in the thought that in my own village the name of Bacha would still be revered. I had done too much for the people of Kalakan lightly for them to turn me aside.

Because of the soldiers who followed, Malik and I tarried long on the hillsides, obtaining a little butter and goat's flesh here, and a few breads there.

Finally, we came to Kalakan, and my heart swelled within me as I thought of the fires and of the roasting goats, and the roistering which would follow my appearance.

Two miles from Kalakan I gave that cry of the highlanders which carries so far in the rarefied atmosphere of the mountains. I stood still, Malik with me, and I knew well that sharp eyes in the village would have recognised our forms even at that distance.

I could see men running in the village street, and my eyes grew bright, for here at least I would be welcome, and I need no longer consider myself a fugitive.

As we advanced, I could see men issuing from the village—a deputation to welcome back the traveller who had been their King and would still be a great and successful raider of the hills.

As I was able to take stock of the men more clearly, I thought that this was a curious home-coming. Ahead marched the Elders, and those who came behind came empty-handed. There was no wild firing of rifles, and the more normal expressions of jubilation and joy.

I heard Malik muttering in his beard.

Half a mile from the village, the group halted, and waited for us to come up, and it was then that I saw the grave mien of the Elders, and was troubled.

Yet: "Oh," I called blithely enough, "Bacha comes among you again."

The Elders rose, and one who was their spokesman pulled at his beard, while he regarded me gravely.

"Oh, Bacha Saquo," he replied sombrely enough, "we give you greetings, but——"

He gazed round at the assembled Elders as if seeking inspiration. The faces were stony, and lacked expression, and with a shrug of his shoulders, he addressed me again.

"Oh, Bacha, we have been awaiting you, but the news which we have to give is not good. We as the Elders have to tell you that your presence here is unwelcome. We would have you, O Bacha, but the decree has gone forth from Kabul, and this new good King must be obeyed. We are unable to offer you sustenance or shelter.

"There are orders," he went on, "that we should apprehend you should you come to our village. But you have not come, Bacha, and we have not seen you.

"There are also orders that he who gives you assistance will be hauled to Kabul as a traitor.

"We give you nothing, Bacha, but each night food and milk will be placed upon the hillsides for anyone who cares to partake.

"This we have considered, Bacha. It grieves us

to take this course, but . . . there is no other way."

Solemnly, the other Elders nodded their beards in agreement. Silently they turned, and wended their way back to the village.

I, Bacha, had not only lost the throne, but I was an outcast from my own home.

CHAPTER XXIV

AGAIN, THE ARG

MALIK and I lived upon the hillsides, and upon the food which was placed there for our succour.

Sometimes, the boy who brought the food, would tarry, and addressing the crags and boulders, would give news. Thus were we able to avoid the troops who continually combed the countryside for us.

Apparently, there was much discussion in Kabul as to my fate. The King, it would seem, would have me pardoned and free to roam the hills as an outcast. But the General Assembly which he had gathered was composed of many men whom I had mulcted of their gold and of many whom I had orphaned.

Seemingly, they thirsted for revenge.

For many days news was scant. Then, Kabul's fiat was known.

We were to be taken at all costs, and death was to be my reward.

I thought little of death. It meant nothing to me, for I had achieved my ambition, and had been King. I had had my way with men, and I had made my mark. The land of Afghanistan would not speedily forget my rule.

But, to die as these people would have me die! That was repugnant.

I would keep to the hillsides, and use of my craft, and avoid these stumbling and cursing Kabulis who rattled over the goat paths searching for the outcast.

But, in making this resolve, I underestimated the power of greed. Large rewards were offered for my capture, and it was unarmed hillmen who eventually took me, and not the sabre-thrusters from Kabul.

Early one morning I saw villagers approaching. I took little heed of them, for they knew I was in the vicinity, and it was their wont silently to pass me by. But these men did not pass. I had used my turban to rest my head, and I was bare-headed when the sense of impending danger came to me.

I saw a man stoop, and pick up a stone. Others followed his example, and a shower of missiles came my way. I replied with gusto, for I could thus kill a bird in flight, but one well-aimed rock caught me on the side of the head and on the place where a brass pot had found its mark when I lived in the bazaars of Peshawar.

All went black, and for several days, so I learned, I knew nothing.

When my senses returned, I was back in Kabul and in the Arg. There was no couch in the Salam Khana for me, but only a charpoi in its deepest dungeon.

I gazed round the stone walls, unable to comprehend at first, but eventually my predicament was borne home to me.

There was a rattling at the door, and a man appeared, bearing a pitcher of water, some milk and curried goat's flesh.

I turned upon him in disdain, for he was a low born.

"What is this?" I cried angrily. "Is this how your King is to be fed?"

The ingrate grinned, but said nothing.

Spurning the food with my foot, I kicked it savagely away.

Loudly as I could, for my voice was weak, I called for the guard.

I recognised the man when he appeared as one who had been of my personal bodyguard. My entrails writhed, such was my chagrin, but I would be the King still, notwithstanding.

"Is it part of your Afghan hospitality," I chided, "that dishonour be heaped on the head of a Royal prisoner?"

This man did not grin. Undoubtedly, he felt his position.

"By whose orders have I been so insulted?" I demanded.

The guard hesitated. "The Captain of the Guard," he replied with some diffidence.

"You will inform the Captain of the Guard that I have a serious complaint to lodge," I retorted, and the man departed.

I know not what happened, but I suspect that word was conveyed to the King, for within half-an-hour more victuals appeared, and the server was a white-coated, white-turbaned bearer.

Two—three—five—six days. I lost count, and I was requested to prepare myself for my court-martial.

Court-martial. I laughed. I could have told the guards the verdict ere I left my cell.

I was hauled into a large chamber—one where
I had spent many pleasant hours deriding those who
were tardy in giving of their wealth—and I was
arraigned as a traitor, a murderer, a thief, a brigand.
The officer who read the indictment became hoarse
of voice before he had concluded the sonorous
wording.

"What say you, Bacha Saquo, son of the water-
carrier of Kalakan . . . guilty, or not guilty?"

I looked round at that semi-circle of hard, un-
smiling faces, and laughed. It was not such a
laugh as one would give when endeavouring to
dissemble. It was a hearty guffaw, for these men
were so serious. They took their task to heart,
and they might have been giving judgment on a
matter of import rather than on an insignificant
trifle—a mere life.

"Guilty, or not guilty?"

The words came again, and the officer who
uttered them was obviously shocked. That a
prisoner should so lightly regard these proceedings
savoured of the indecorous and unseemly.

"Your answer!"

I spat upon the carpet, and gazed down at the
mess of saliva.

I inclined my head.

My answer was there for all to see.

A ripple of anger and of astonishment went
round the room, and I heard the president gasp.

I could afford to grin. I still had my hour, and
I still possessed the power to rile these men.

I gazed out of the windows to the smashed
ramparts beyond. I studied the decorations of the

ceiling. I allowed my eyes to follow the delicate patterns of the carpet. But to these men's words I paid no attention. They might not have been there, and—in truth they bored me. The outcome of their foolish phrasing was known. Why this avalanche of talk?

At length it was over.

To die.

To face a firing squad on a date to be determined.

Again the cell.

The end, but not an unfitting end to a life such as mine.

I would have loathed the cages, and the slow march of death through thirst and starvation. . . . Starvation, perhaps. But, thirst—no! I should have hated the poles of the aerodrome, the painful ascent, and the sudden impaling, but I would not have been unhappy had the sentence been a sudden exit before a cannon.

But this was better than I anticipated.

A firing squad!

There is ever a certain dignity. . . .

POSTSCRIPT

THERE was a certain difficulty attaching to the demise of Bacha Saquo and those who were sentenced with him, for such was the abhorrence with which he was regarded that not even gravediggers could be found who would besmirch themselves by touching his body.

On the morning set for his execution, he was roused early, and told that he must prepare for his death.

Again Bacha Saquo laughed, and spat at the man who conveyed the tidings.

He was offered clean raiment, but he spurned the gesture, preferring to face the firing squad in the tatters which had been his when he was taken in his own hills.

When he arrived at the execution ground, he found a long, deep trench already dug, and as the principal culprit, he was placed on the extreme left. On his right, and ranged at suitable intervals, were those who had been his principal executioners and torturers during the nine months of his turbulent reign.

He was made to kneel, and he was given time to make his peace with Allah, and he spent a long time in gazing around him.

Those whose task it was to carry through the ceremony reminded him that his last hour had come, but again this strange man laughed, even in the face of an ignominious death.

"I do not require you to tell me that," he replied pertly, as if he were exchanging badinage round his own village fire. "It has been decreed . . . it is Kismet."

"But," a Mullah expostulated, "why do you not pray. Why do you not raise your hands in supplication, making these, your last requests?"

Bacha Saquo was actually amused, even with his grave yawning behind him.

"Why should I raise my hands to Allah?" he taunted. "He has given me all that I have desired. I have been King. I have had my every ambition realised. What more is there for me to ask?"

He glanced along the line of doomed men, all of whom were praying devoutly.

"How long," he demanded, "is this sorry farce to continue? I thought I was coming here to be shot. It seems that I am but an exhibition for the curious!"

With an outraged shrug of his shoulders, the Mullah turned away, and conferred with the officer in charge of the firing parties.

The officer nodded in the direction of the still bowing figures, and his expression was eloquent.

Bacha Saquo might deride death. He might even welcome it. But—he would have to wait for it. All must be conducted with decorum and precision. Merely because he was Bacha he could not be accorded a volley out of his turn.

Eventually, however, the last of the praying figures had risen to its feet, and the long line of drooping heads gazed forlornly at the array of soldiers.

Not so Bacha. His head twisted and turned, and he made ribald jest with the unresponsive man next to him.

The order went along the line:

"Firing parties . . . load!"

"Firing parties . . . steady!"

"Firing parties . . . on your targets!"

"Firing parties . . . ready!"

Then Bacha laughed.

A sword flashed downwards, and the riflemen followed the signal.

There was a crashing volley, followed by three belated shots which came incongruously to the ear.

One by one that line of men sank downwards and backwards, to fall, untidily, and with limbs awry, into the trench.

The last so to disappear, was Bacha. His resistance to death must have been amazing.

And, the last picture:

Men with shovels, groaning and sweating.

A long mound of newly rammed earth.

The last of a King, and—in one's ears, that eerie laugh still ringing.